ALMA MATER

Books by HENRY SEIDEL CANBY

ALMA MATER

THE GOTHIC AGE OF THE AMERICAN COLLEGE

BY

HENRY SEIDEL CANBY

ILLUSTRATED BY CHARLES W. SMITH

FARRAR & RINEHART

INCORPORATED

ON MURRAY HILL   NEW YORK

CONTENTS

PREFACE

The self-made, self-taught man, greedy for power, set his mark on the nineties, and it was after his industrial triumphs that the small-town culture of that confident American age began to decay. But it is the college graduate who has imposed his codes, his ideals, and his personality upon our twenties and thirties. His way of life was settled in a college experience which for power over the imagination has had few equals since the monastic period. It was a youthful adventure, a shallow culture, a set of ideals vague and seldom critical, and for his real thinking, often his real motives, the undergraduate waited or went elsewhere. Yet it was an intense experience. In spite of the numerous books upon American education in the nineties and early nineteen hundreds I can find none that adequately describes it, or relates the college of that day to youth as I knew it. They deal with the facts better than I can, since they are broader in scope, but they leave out the immensely important element of emotion. The college I write of here was more than an institution, it was a community with a vital life of its own, a state within the state.

And just as the typical American of the nineties was a small-town man, so the dominant American type of our thirties is college bred. He chiefly, but also she, has been conditioned by the unique circumstances of a curious society, part training-ground for a ruthless competition, part cloister, part romance. There has never been anything quite like the American college of the turn of the twentieth century, never any institution more confused in its purposes, more vital, more mixed in its ideals, more loved. It is the theme of this book, which is a personal record of what it was, what it did to us, what powerful hands it laid upon the United States of our generations. Of course, not all of America went to college, by no means necessarily the best of America went to college. Nevertheless, if it had not been for the conflict between college life and so-called college education, if the college had been differently adjusted to the economic, the intellectual, and most of all to the emotional growth of the country, then I believe that we should have been today another nation, perhaps better, perhaps worse, certainly different.

Preface

I make no pretense here of encyclopedic knowledge or of breadth of experience. This book, like its predecessor, "The Age of Confidence," is a contribution to history, not history itself, which it is much too early to write. It is a study in memory, a critical memoir of a long college experience in a time of change when sometimes the college moved faster and sometimes the country. It is an estimate of values, often appreciative, often critical, but personal always without being rigorously autobiographical, and it relies upon experience recalled and freely interpreted for its validity. It can be little broader than that experience, which was largely at one college. Yet it can go deeper for there is a perspective in the writing of from twenty to thirty years. I fear that it is inexcusably masculine, considering the importance of the woman's college and the woman graduate and undergraduate in these decades, but that is a misfortune of sex not of intention, and in most of these pages what is said of man applies equally to woman. Memory, however, must take its evidence where it can find it. I have taught girls often, but I have never been one.

That the first two decades of this century

were outstanding in American college life I assert with some confidence, because they were an era of sharpest transition in the country at large. Beginning in the late nineties with the romantic age of college life in full and somewhat fantastic flower, these years stretch on to and beyond that curious turning-point in the nineteen tens when America, in common with Western culture, began to grow realistic, critical, and doubtful of the future. They reach to the end of the war and the beginning of what was so clearly a new era as to need no argument. They include the triumph of applied science, the breakdown of stereotyped religion, the defeat of the classics in American education, and the dramatic appearance, full blown, of American confidence in our own scholarship and our own literature. They saw the collegiate youth rise, strut, and decline into the comics. All this is true, and yet my chief reason for writing of this Gothic age of college life is, that it was then that I knew it, loved it, hated it, struggled in it, and took it deep into my imagination.

I have known many American colleges, but only one well. That does not, I truly believe, affect the justice of what I have to say. Harvard was old Harvard, as the song says, when Yale was but a pup, and of a different breed. The most ardent believer in standardization would not dare to assert that college life among the lakes of Wisconsin was identical with experience in a Princeton dormitory or upon a Southern campus. The differences, however, were unimportant when compared with the resemblances, and though each body of undergraduates boasted of an exclusive distinction in manners, clothes, slang, morale, outlook, and even in personality, and each faculty regarded itself as marked by an intellectual individualism in the eyes of the world, yet this outside world knew only a "student" and a "professor" who fitted very readily into types.

Furthermore, the younger colleges, whether they were "state" or "privately endowed" institutions, modeled their life and aspirations upon the older colleges, which were usually in the East, and which drew heavily from the best schools and the wealthiest or most cultivated classes. Fashions began there and spread, so that a new twist to a hat brim or a new method of teaching traveled in a few years from ocean to ocean, and gave a unity to college life. I am not writing here of that larger organization of professional schools, service bureaus, and organs of scholarship, called a university. There history was differently made. But the American college for undergraduates ran true to form, if infinitely varied in secondary characteristics, all round the states. Its peculiar life was most highly developed in the men's colleges, which inherited the traditions (not all of them decorous) of monasticism, least developed in co-educational institutions, yet whatever the differentiation, the tailor who first adopted the word "collegiate" for his wares was a shrewd fellow. In the early nineteen hundreds both the college undergraduate and the college graduate could be easily recognized in their communities. They belonged to a class that was far more homogeneous than America at large.

From these campuses, which even in my day had begun to go Gothic in their architecture, came many, if not most, of the two generations of Americans who now are in executive charge of the country, and the greater part of the codes, ideals, manners, and ideals of living which dominate us. Here was the conditioning laboratory for the most promising of our impressionable youth. These were the Utopias from which they emerged to tackle with extraordinary confidence, only recently shaken, a country which was becoming a social and economic problem while they fought for the prizes of their little college world.

ALMA MATER

CHAPTER I

The College Town

I REMEMBER first the college town. Surely it is amazing that neither history, nor sociology, nor fiction, has given more than passing attention to the American college town, for surely it has had a character and a personality unlike other towns. And quite as surely, its imprint of small-town respectability, convention, and common sense, is deeper upon American education than has ever been guessed. With the rarest exceptions the home of the college has been a small town, even if that town was a suburb or a section, self-contained, of a city. There were hundreds of such towns in the period of which I write, and all with a family resemblance.

Cleaner, neater than other towns, with green spaces somewhere toward the center, and white spires or Gothic towers or windowed dormitories half hid by trees, they were little capitals of the academic state. As trading or industrial centers their life might be indistinguishable from towns or cities of a like size, but in their social consciousness there was always some recognition of peculiarity. For the heart of the community was a college. Its subtle influences were as pervasive if less noticeable than the quite unsubtle symbols of college life—playing fields, cafés, and collegiate clothing.

And in the early nineteen hundreds the college town was no luncheon stop for automobiles. It was secluded, even if it was a town within a city, like the New Haven of Yale; it knew its boundaries and kept them, it was jealous of its distinctions, if it was uneasy it was also proud. The campus and the college buildings dominated its architecture like the temple and citadel of a Greek city state, a difficult relationship since there was always some doubt in the minds of the town folk whether the college was an asset or a parasite. The town with its college was like a woman's club committee with a celebrity in tow, a credit to them but also an embarrassment and sometimes a nuisance; it was like a French village built upon a Roman camp to which tourists

resort; it was like the mistress of an actors'
boarding-house, pleased by the notoriety but
worried by the manners, or the morals, of her
boarders; it was like almost anything but a town
without a college. And many a college town
was like a resentful mother who, expecting a
quiet and manageable infant, had given birth to
a Gargantua that swallowed whole streets and
squares in its gigantic growing. I do not wish
to be fantastic, yet only such similes will express
how very unlike the rest of the United States was
the college town. Its nature was conditioned
by the college, of which it was the irritable but
fostering mother.

New Haven, as I first knew it in the late nineties, was a decorous and beautiful town, set in
the midst of a sprawling industrial city of slums,
factories, and long, undistinguished avenues.
The college town was old New Haven, with its
Green, its bordering business streets, its campus
and north-stretching blocks of residences with
park and country beyond. The elm-shaded
streets of this old town were lined by sedate
houses which in various modes still kept the
impress of the Greek revival of the early nineteenth century. Eight out of ten had a portico

of wood with two Doric columns painted brown or gray or white. Down the length of shady streets these columns made a pleasant arcade, broken here and there by high brick mansions of the eighties, or a charming green-shuttered, white-walled reminder of the better proportions of a Colonial day. This college town was the ego of the city of New Haven.

It was a guarded town, very unlike the ample if ugly spaciousness of the mansarded avenues of my youth to the southward, where broad porches and open gates welcomed relatives and friends. There were no open doors in the New England college town. Behind the twin Doric columns, which might have been labeled Respectability and Reserve, two squint lights seemed always to be looking down their noses at the passerby, fearful lest he should wish to enter. The college town, unlike the rest of America, was jealous of privacy, and doubtful of casual relationships.

Lights went out early in these bosky streets, often to be relit in upstairs studies. When the chapel bell rang ten, while the undergraduate navigating homeward across the Green filled the night with shouts and melody, the prim town pulled up its covers, shut its ears, or burrowed deeper in a book. Nights in the college town were consecrated to sleep or work.

Along these town streets, professors lived, students wandered, but also the social and professional leaders of the city sought residence because, after all, it was the college that gave tone to the community. Academic society was therefore both town and gown, and had a double flavor which recalled in homely fashion the atmosphere of those small European courts where prince and bishop each had their following. It was not an exciting society, yet certainly it was not dull. New Haven had never forgotten that it was once a colony, all of itself, and might have been a state had it not sheltered republicans and regicides. There was a stiff, aristocratic quality in the old families, now entirely lost there as elsewhere in America. From their harsh stalks sprouted personalities of extraordinary independence, so that it was hard to tell sometimes whether decorum or eccentricity was the dominant note of the town's society. These families belonged to the college world yet were not wholeheartedly of it. They arranged its finances, fought its lawsuits, supplied a president or a professor now and then, were mysteriously powerful sometimes in academic affairs, yet in general their attitude of respectful but slightly contemptuous toleration of learning, so characteristic of America, was tempered only by the belief that the college belonged to them and put them a cut above the aristocracies of Hartford or Springfield, and made them able to take rank even in New York. Hence the teacher who in this money-making age lived on the edge or beyond of society, in the college town might have a definite place, though he was not society himself. Wealth and position did not so much stoop to him as restrain their privileges so that he could enter. By a self-denying ordinance, tacitly understood, the rich in the college set (and no other society counted) spent only a part of their incomes at home, eschewed butlers, denied themselves broughams, and later, for a while, automobiles, kept dues low in the clubs, and, if they did spend, put their money into that good wine and costly food which the scholar has always enjoyed. And he responded with an unexpected geniality which was sometimes grateful and sometimes lumbering, and sometimes only a courteous irony.

Thus the college was privileged socially, not only in the hand-picked sons of the cultivated or the well-to-do that came as students, but in the close contacts between the faculty and the aristocracy of the college town. But it was limited and conditioned also by the life of a small-town community, which no matter how good its traditions, how admirable its character, how genuine its culture, was, by definition, a little provincial, a little priggish, and very much inbred. And yet there was a raciness in this mingling of town and gown that gave its own flavor to the college society, and was some compensation for the gustier airs which blew through capitals and metropolises.

I can see now a characteristic "reception" in a great house behind the broad sweep of the elms of Hillhouse Avenue, which was to the college town of New Haven what upper Park Avenue is to New York—a terminus of social pride. Tables were laden with heavy, mind-satisfying food, champagne bubbled on the sideboards, stiff-backed professors were trying to relax, while their wives, with the curious pursed mouth of the academic woman, showed more concern for their dignity than for the entertainment.

Among them moved the grand dames of our town society, soothing vanities by a kind word, snubbing with a vacant look the strange uncouth creatures that science was bringing into the university, but not too emphatically since one never knew nowadays who might become famous. And with them were our town eccentrics, women usually of old families, too sure of themselves to bother about social distinctions. Worse dressed than the professors' wives, they had a confident distinction of ugliness which lifted them above our small-town limitations, and they spoke the language of the academic world with understanding and tolerance, like missionaries among an Indian tribe. Trailing behind them, yet always heading back toward the champagne, were our faculty "characters" —the great hearty souls that scholarship which is not pedantry creates in its happier moods, men whose broadcloth might be shiny and spotted, their linen none too clean, yet with minds and faces of the great world, known in Europe and conscious of it, witty often, sarcastic usually, ill mannered, inclined to lash out at this pompous bourgeois society, which nevertheless gave them their only chance to eat, drink, and be merry with their own kind. There was our famous Chaucerian scholar, Lounsbury, his sparse white beard wagging under his rapid tongue, his eyes a little bleary, his imagination, lit from history, making a marquise out of old Mrs. Dusenberry, and a clown of our leading banker. "Why do you want to put old Whitney's name on the courthouse wall? All he knew was Sanskrit. What did he ever do for New Haven?" says the banker. "Do!" Lounsbury shoots back, "By Gorry! It's enough that he lived here!"

There were subtle jealousies between town and gown which could not be assigned to differences in income. The town had inherited a Yankee distrust of ministers who talked about God but made no money, and now that ministers were less and professors more it transferred this distrust with increments. It was irritated by its own deference to an institution that did not live for profits. Energy that in other communities was organizing machine tools or life insurance, here in this college community leaked away in a trickle that sometimes carried sons and heirs with it into the academic world where it was transformed into the teaching of adolescents or into books that nobody but professors read. The town derived a goodly share of its income from the rapidly increasing expenditures of the college and its students, and this too it resented, feeling that it was committed to an approval of what the college was doing. It endured the noisy night life of the students, the untidy boarding houses that crowded its streets, the arrogance of the academic mind, but it disliked the haunting sense of inferiority which came from knowing that it was celebrated because of the college. It listened to the endless shop-talk of the faculty and pretended to take the "big men" of the undergraduate world at their face value, but it could not entirely respect, and still less understand, the creature upon which it lived and which it believed it had created. Not until the expansive twenties (beyond the scope of this book) when alumni enriched by the war and prosperity upset their apple carts of gold into the college coffers, and made education, or at least the side-shows of education, a big business, was the town convinced that the college, its own college, was worthy of its birthplace. No Commencement orator was ever so persuasive as gifts in the millions and a building program that was a major industry.

And yet, as with Christians and Infidels living together in old Spain, there was more interpenetration than appeared on the surface. The college taught the town to discuss ideas, it taught also friendship and a delight in the companionship of like-minded men. The two blended in the adult life of the community, for the habit of the undergraduate fraternity persisted in dozens of little clubs of talkers which flourished throughout the town because their members had learned clubability. It was a rash hostess who gave a dinner party on Wednesday or Friday nights, their favorite meeting times. In these clubs scholar, lawyer, and business man met, ate, drank, and read papers explaining their jobs or their social philosophy. Ideas spread through the college town, freed from that taboo on abstractions which was the curse of the small town elsewhere in America, and many a scholar was saved from pedantry, or a paralysis of the emotions in the arid wastes of specialist theory, by his contacts with men whose daily task was the handling of men. Even the women became clubable; and indeed it was in New Haven that by happy inspiration Our Society was born, whose inestimable privilege it was to talk first and then inspect every closet in their hostess's house. But it was a man's town.

Still another institution the college gave to the society of the town, the college widow. I knew two of them in their old age and profited greatly from my friendship with them. For the college widow had a depth and richness of emotional experience never developed in American life of that day outside of the few metropolises, and seldom there. She began at sixteen or eighteen, as a ravishing beauty, the darling of freshmen; she passed on in the years of her first blooming from class to class of ardent youngsters, until, as her experience ripened, she acquired a taste, never to be satisfied by matrimony, for male admiration, abstracted from its consequences; and more subtly, for the heady stimulant of intimacy with men in their fresh and vigorous youth. By her thirties she had learned the art of eternal spring, and had become a connoisseur in the dangerous excitement of passion controlled at the breaking point, a mistress of every emotion, and an adept in the difficult task of sublimating love into friendship. The students lived out their brief college life and went on; she endured, and tradition with her, an enchantress in illusion and a specialist in the heart. Twenty, even thirty years, might be her tether; and when suddenly on a midnight, a shock of reality, or perhaps only boredom, ended it all, she was old—but still charming and infinitely wise. To smoke a cigarette with her when cigarettes were still taboo for women, and drink her coffee and liqueur, was a lesson in civilization.

Yet in fostering in its midst the sprawling infant, gray-headed but still growing, which was the college, the town sacrificed its own youth. There was childhood and maturity in a college town, but no youth in between. Youth male was absorbed into the undergraduate community and came home only on Sundays, youth female was usually sent off perforce to school or woman's colleges, away from the dangerous glamour of college streets. Hence the young folk in the college town settled back into their home environment only in their mid or late twenties, and then only did social life in a community begin for them. There were no calf loves in the society of the college town, no gawkish immaturity, no giggling, no rebellious escapes. And since the young had reached the earning and marrying stage in a society where the scale of living was based for them upon an instructor's salary (in those days $1000 to $1500 a year), their pleasures were necessarily simple. Relative poverty was regarded as a virtue, doing without was a pride. One walked not rode, went to concerts rather than to the theatre, danced to a piano and a cornet, gave books not jewelry, sat down four at a table not eight, kept married instead of toying with expensive ideas about lovers and divorce.

The results for the college town were by no means ill. The tittle-tattle of a small town had little fuel here. It was an educated society, and since it could not afford to be frivolous, and both Puritan custom and economy held the passions in check, every opportunity was given to vivacity and ideas in conversation. Talk was cheap, which did not prevent it from being good. It was often stiff with convention and sometimes pedantical, yet the fun was more civilized than country-club horseplay, the wit, when any, aware of the nature of wit.

And yet it was all a little arid. The young people had come together too late. They had no sentimental memories to share, and thanks to the restrictions of what was, after all, a small town, and to the official nature of their college society, and to relative poverty, the sex in relationships was weak. Every emotion had its inhibition. Like the columns of the houses, the twin shrines in every heart were Reserve and Respectability.

I have written of the college town of the Gothic age with pleasure because I was happy there, and excited, and amused, and also cabin'd, cribb'd, confined; yet also with a very definite purpose. For it is impossible to think of the college of that day without its encircling town. This was the air the professor breathed, and which the student absorbed from his freshman year onward. For him the town often provided his first experience in adult social life. Nor in discussing the internal conflicts of the college itself which have been so decisive in shaping the type known as the college graduate, is it right to forget for a moment the influence of these nests of Puritan respectability, given tone by the American aristocracy that clung to them for shelter from the make-money world outside. Here is a factor in education and in the faiths and prejudices of the educated and the educator which has escaped the theorist and the statistician alike. We have forgotten that the types we analyze so readily—professors, alumni, humanists, scientists, scholars—were in their conditioning period American boys in a small college town.

Well there it was, the college town, and still is, I suppose, although it must have lost much of the pleasant flavor of social provincialism blended with the free intellect which I knew; and although I have written frankly of New Haven I believe that my description would fit, with unimportant changes of custom and circumstance, a hundred college towns of the period. Also I have written badly if I have not made clear that in this best of situations for reconciling the man of theory and the man of practice, the characteristic American fear of ideas and the expert in general, still held fast. The influence of gown upon town and of town upon gown was, when all is said, still indecisive. In clubs, such as our excellent town club of those days, it created an amenity of life and conversation which I have seldom seen equalled. And yet it did not go deep. The two waters did not mix. A boy of a commercial or legal

family who went into the faculty was lost to
his line, taking on a psychology so different
from his brother who had stayed in the family
affairs as to cause remark even among the un-
observant. Whereas a professor's son who went
into business seemed to drop overnight all feeling and often all respect for the craft of teaching and scholarship.

The college town was thus the imperfect resultant of two worlds in a physical merger,
whose souls and minds remained disparate.
That, I think, was a tragedy of American education. Perhaps some equivalent antinomy has
been the tragedy of all education. And this
attempted merger was frustrated by another
heterogeneity. The undergraduates by and
large belonged to the faction of the gown, but
had themselves come in a vast majority from
other and uncollegiate small towns, and so were
in ideas and attitudes toward learning far closer
to the Philistines of the streets than to the
Israelites of the campus faculty. The studentry
was a faction within our college body, which
constantly practised direct warfare or passive
resistance against its superiors, usually with the
sneaking sympathy of both parents and town.

Hence there was a split in the college itself, so that in my days not a duality but a trinity—town, gown, and sweater—would have best described our community.

But I run ahead of my argument. This college town was the egg in which nestled the college yolk. Sedate, self-conscious, a little arrogant, surprisingly tolerant of student vices, since it had to live with them, the town that I knew so well arouses in the memory a singular blend of respect, impatience, affection, and irony. It was, after all, high-minded and never trivial, though sometimes mean. The airs of intellectualism that blew about its streets, which themselves had academic dignity and a beauty that was austere though sometimes prim, and its deference to those who had to live plainly in pursuit of their non-profit-making careers, made it very difficult, too difficult, to leave for another environment. And yet because it was not a capital, not really a city, but a small town in which the often limitless intellectual ambitions of a college were walled, there was a liability to such jealousies, to such agonies of hope deferred, to such frustrations, as are known only to those who are caught in a trap and do not know how to get out. The American college, for good and for ill, was moulded and conditioned by the nature and practice of the small town.

CHAPTER II

College Life

WHEN I first saw the college town it was late September and I, a somewhat frightened boy from home, was dragging a suit-case full of books across the exciting spaces of the Green. The books were for the final cram before entrance examinations, but that was only a cold trepidation hung somewhere near my heart, which was warmed by very different emotions. Coming from a small city that had never tried to be Athens, my naive imagination had conceived of a college as an assemblage of Parthenons and cathedrals. What I saw before me that afternoon across the Green would have been disillusioning if I had been realistic. The rather dingy halls, boxes ornamented with pseudo Gothic or Byzantine, were little like my dream, and the beautifully simple relics of the old college of brick Colonial were much too simple to mean anything

[23]

to my taste tutored in the nineties. But I was far from being realistic, so that in a second of time, between Green and campus, I had dropped, with the easy inconsequentiality of youth, all illusions of architectural grandeur for the real thing, college life.

Viewed backward from our nineteen thirties, this college life which was to make such an imprint on the behavior and the ideals of the leaders of the oncoming generation, looms up, a cloud of influences, sometimes rich, sometimes sinister, sometimes trivial. Close at hand or described from memory, it seemed more like a haven for American youth, a little space of time in which energy had its outlet, and where the young made a world to suit themselves, which, for a while at least, the adult world was to accept at surprisingly near the college estimate.

This much I had heard, although in language much less philosophical; and therefore a glamour hung over the college town and the college at its heart, which was not to abate but rather to increase its enchantments, on past the climax of senior year. Thousands like myself (so I felt as I crossed the Green) had been there before me in a life which was to become my experience.

At home most of us, and certainly I myself, had lived in one dimension, with at most a family extension toward an American past. Overnight we were to step through an opening door into tradition, a usable, sympathetic tradition of youth. It was to be our privilege to be born again, painlessly, and without introspection. All this, which I felt, not spoke, was true.

Therefore, like all that confident generation, I accepted the college as I found it, and believed in its life and its spirit with a fanatic devotion. I saw that the boys who were strolling that day in the latter nineties down the autumn streets were as easily distinguishable among the town crowds as beings from another world. The town was only their background, and I picked them out in their turtle-neck sweaters under the briefest of top coats, as a dog sees only other dogs on a busy road. There was an arrogant and enchanting irresponsibility in their behavior which was intoxicating. I longed to get rid of my suitcase with its irrelevant books, and into a sweater which I saw to be obligatory—to dress like them, be like them.

A few nights later I was herded with other freshmen into a straggling parade, which

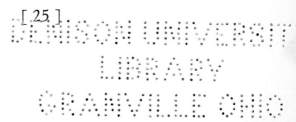

marched to a space of torch-light and confusion where champions wrestled for the honor of their classes. And there were the Strong Silent Men I had read about in the newspapers, the football and crew heroes, calming the crowded field by the full-breasted dignity of the white letters on their blue sweaters. And there were other slighter figures in tiny top coats with upturned collars, who seemed to exercise an equal authority. These, I was told, were the Big Men, the managers, the powers behind college life, more important, because brainier, than the athletes. These were the real masters of this new state. I felt, in a leap of the imagination, as if I were being naturalized into a new government, more vital than any I had known, as indeed I was.

It was 1896, at the very crisis of one of the few bitter and doubtful political struggles of my time in America. Bryan had nailed capitalism on his cross of gold and was touring the enemy East in what then seemed a triumphal career. He spoke on the Green, and we students (how warmly I called myself by that name) thronged a thousand or so, milling about among the townsfolk but conscious, as always, only of ourselves. I remember with ironic emphasis how my curiosity as to the appearance of the Great Commoner was forgotten in a deeper thrill when I found myself pressed in the crowd against one of the "Big Men" of the night before, who was actually asking me, "What did he say? Could you hear?"

There was shouting and booing, hissing and applause. The students were heavily against Bryan. I felt that, but also that it was no active opposition, but only a reaction to what they had heard from home. He did not belong in their world. We were excited, and a little amused, by such a stirring of the dull adult population over matters that concerned us only a little.

My class was the entering one of 1899. "Ninety-nine out of a hundred," boomed the Great Commoner from his platform in the midst of the swirling mob, "ninety-nine out of a hundred of the students in this university are sons of the idle rich."

Perhaps it was not quite that, although certainly this was the sentiment he expressed. Did it matter? He had said the magic word, the rallying numeral. If the students had booed and whooped with the crowd before, now they shouted. "Ninety-nine!" "Nine-nine-ninety-nine," a chorus took it up, seniors beginning, freshmen, recognizing their symbol, joining in. "Nine, nine, ninety-nine." It seemed to be a scurrilous attack of economic parasites upon a statesman of the people, and so the Democratic papers from coast to coast reported it the next morning. Actually it was nothing of the sort. We were too innocent to know what economic parasitism was, and indeed we were no more parasitical than any other youngsters in the educational period, and far from idle. Our chanted impertinence was only the automatic response of a society that knew no politics or economics but its own, to one of its passwords, uttered by accident. We were like a savage tribe who sees their totem embroidered on the flag of an explorer.

Years afterwards I met Bryan, who well remembered this episode, but I could not persuade him that it was college life not the bias of the idle rich which drowned his speech in mirth and yelling. Yet that was the true explanation. I had entered a state within a state, and joined a faction of that state, the student body, aware really only of themselves, their own life, their own ideals. Nor did we guess how closely an umbilical cord attached us to the energy of our country.

The first sensation in this new world was of a wholly delightful irresponsibility. It was a one-way irresponsibility only, since we were deeply responsible to the *mores* of our college world, yet so far as home and town and the world outside generally were concerned, it was like release from confinement, boredom, or pain. We kicked up our heels in that pleasant college town like colts in a pasture. It was a somewhat rowdy irresponsibility, so the town thought, which liked to bawl at night under respectable windows, smash lamp-post glass with beer bottles, and hock best suits for an evening's pleasure, scorning decorum. These childish tricks, which, I am told, are scorned as "collegiate" by a new university generation, were only symptoms of our independence from home rules and school discipline. They were one sign that we had got a franchise in living, another being the egregious bad taste with which we furnished our rooms with cigar-ribbon pillows, bad chromos of girls in the college color, and "Turkish corners" bought entire at a department store. Among the more intellectual the same desire for self-assertion subscribed for de luxe sets of Maupassant, Balzac, or Thackeray, which seldom got finally paid for.

This rebellion against decorum and the customs of dull every day had its romance and its poetry. It was scurrilous but not insolent, bawdy but not obscene. I find its careless, happy irresponsibility best preserved in a Yale folk song of the nineties, author unknown, which I believe has never before been put in print. The scene is on Thursday or Saturday night, the setting a long table with steins and pretzels, the dramatis personæ two companies of students, ranged on either side. The ship mentioned is the old *Richard Peck,* once of boisterous fame, that ran nightly from New Haven to New York, the time is 11 P. M., the mood neither drunken nor sober, the spirit that of "Down with Respectability, drink her down." Choruses answer each other across the table.

Invitation from the Right

I will tell you of a little scheme I've got,
And I hope, sirs, that you will refuse it not,

College Life

To go down upon the Richard Peck tonight,
And have fun aplenty in the moo-oon light.

Acceptance from the Left

We accept your generous invitation,
Since having pleasure is our occupation.
We will meet you on the dock at twelve o'clock,
And to get the dough we'll put our watch and
*   chain in hock.*

Chorus, Both Sides

Oh, we will have the hell of a time, I'll tell you
*   what,*
Loving, lushing, stowing wine into our faces.
And we'll sit up till the morning and enjoy the
*   light of dawning,*
Hully Gee!, by God, we'll raise hell on the Peck!
*   Diddly Dum,*
*   Take my advice,*
*   Diddly Dum,*
*   On the Peck.*

Of course all this was just youthful exuber-
ance of animal high spirits, shot through, except
for the grossest, with that traditional romance
of student life which has come down to us un-
broken from the medieval university, its vagabond students, the Goliards, its arrogant unre-

spectability. The real irresponsibility went much deeper, was in fact both an escape and a new allegiance. It was the boy's escape from his duty to be conformist in his own family and respectable in his home town. It was an escape (though he would never have so phrased it) from dull bourgeois life, with its emphasis upon being businesslike and timeserving to relatives or employers. Or it was a breakaway from the moral platitudes and conventional discipline of boarding school. All this the freshman eluded by a bound into a community where the mirth and the energy he best understood were sanctioned by a powerful public opinion, and had their immediate rewards; where he could make his personality prevail if he had one; where his age was the right age, while on the horizon hung grandiose possibilities which, realized, would bring him home the boy that made good, carrying glamour with him.

A longing to escape from the inferiorities of childhood and to triumph over the elders who think that they are betters, is, and has been, of course, common to all youth. Therefore the freshman changed his tie, his hat, his slang, as a manifesto of his escape from rule, but also of his new allegiance. He was no longer a boy from Rochester, he was a Princeton undergraduate, admitted to the rights and privileges of college life, and this consciousness went to the roots of his being, making him sensitive to every push and pull of his new environment, and therefore intensely aware of the public opinion of his new society, which again like a Greek city state, was simple, homogeneous in its unity, diverse in personnel, stratified socially, proud, vain, and supremely confident of its way of life. It is impossible to describe truly those shady streets of "eating joints" and rooming houses, those bleak college halls, the cocky students, playing ball like boys on the campus grass, laughing, teasing, yet tense when their mood was serious, unless one remembers that under its aspect of flaunted carelessness this was a well-knit community, intensely self-conscious, in which emotions were easily stirred toward comedy or tragedy,—a community that defined its own success, pursued it constantly, and was arrogantly indifferent to the ideals of others, asking its members for complete and wholehearted allegiance. That parody of a parody,

"The Son of a Gambolier," which we used to sing tramping home at midnight:—

What the hell do we care, what the people say,
We are, we are, we are, we are the Yale Y. M.
    C. A.,

was not so much a scoff at Christian piety as a characteristic expression of the student mind, which pretended to be flippant in everything but college loyalty. It was the first line that was shouted loudest because it voiced the triumph of escape from the tame communities of the home towns.

It was the new loyalty that we felt most deeply, although our escape into self-expression was, of course, a joy in itself. We did cast off very thoroughly the bonds that tied us to the smug, the censorious, and the utilitarian; and so made a limited Utopia. Thoreau, in his way, did much the same when he escaped from the pressure of greed, and of responsibility to a society of which he did not approve, into the leafy solitudes of Walden. He went there to work as a poor student, with high thinking as his goal. We, comfortable and careless scholars, were racing after pleasure and social prestige. Yet I cannot think of that life now except with affection, in spite of its shams, its false values, and its isolation from most worldly realities except the need for competition. To let the whole being go in a frenzy of excitement at a Big Game; to lounge whole evenings through under the wistaria blooms that swung inward over our window seat; to talk endlessly of this and that, vague ideas and rambling argument hiding enthusiasm, trepidation, or desire; to be privileged beings always joking about experience, which we touched lightly because life was still a fascinating experiment—this was not trivial just because what we felt or said seems trivial now. What frankness, for we had little to conceal! What fresh perceptions, for we had seen so little! What confidence, since the difference between success and failure seemed still to be an accident which a push could avoid! And those moonlights, marching home from our mild carouses, hearts released in convivial expansiveness, singing—

And if it be a girl, sir, we'll dress her up in blue,
And send her out to Saltonstall to coach the
  freshman crew,—

or, if the mood was sentimental—

Only a bluebell, emblem of con-stanc-y,
O'er life's wear-y ways, bringing her back to me.
A hundred fathoms, hunder-ed fathoms deep.

That was all an absolute good, a value, giving to the undergraduate of those days a sense of happiness in the simple emotions of friendship which he was not to lose.

In all this we of the early nineties and nineteen hundreds were like the students of every fortunate age. They have always made their own world, and their own ways for it, and their own ideals which, whether worldly or unworldly, have had the short-term quality of youth. But the American experience of my generation differed in some important respects. No weight of political or religious responsibility hung over our community, as upon the reforming, revolutionary, or reactionary student bodies of other times and countries. We were naively yet arrogantly aware that we belonged to America's golden girls and boys, and had been sent to this pleasant place to work a little and play hard, until our time came. Yet, quite unaware, we were actually in the grip of the time-spirit and the local gods of our country. A philosophy bred of Protestantism and pioneering was pricking us hard. The conventional idea (and ours) of the college as a well-organized country club was quite erroneous. There never was a more strenuous preparation for active life anywhere than in the American college of those days. Our illusion of independence was perfect, but it was an illusion.

We were strenuous without thought to ask the reason why. For all but the congenitally lazy, the songful hours over beer steins, the country walks, and the midnights of intimate talk, were interludes (like our lessons) in a tense activity. The cry in our undergraduate world was always "do something," "what does he *do?*" Freshmen hurried up and down entry stairs seeking news for the college paper, athletes, often with drawn, worried faces, struggled daily to get or hold places on the teams, boys with the rudiments of business ability were managers of magazines, orchestras, teams, or co-operative pants-pressing companies. Those who had a voice sang, not for sweet music's sake, but to "make" the glee club. Long throats went in for social drinking glib minds for politics; everything but scholarship was in my day an "activity," and called "doing something for the college." Fraternities read off each meeting night their record of successful achievements, where credit for study meant only that the brethren had kept out of trouble with the faculty. Brother Jones is left guard on the scrub; Brother Smith is "heeling" (expressive term) religion in the Y. M. C. A.; Brother Brown is being urged to write jokes for the Record; Brother Robinson is manager of the chess team. Some voice seemed always to be saying, "Work, for the night is coming." The toil was supposed to be fun, but the rewards were serious. No one that I remember did anything that was regarded as doing, for its own sake. No, the goal was prestige, social preferment, a senior society which would be a springboard to Success in Life. And all gilded, made into illusion, by the theory that in such strenuosity we demonstrated loyalty to our society, which was the college, that thus the selfish man transcended his egoistic self-seekings, and "did" something for Harvard, or Amherst, or Yale.

I think it all bore some resemblance to the frontier of a generation earlier, and perhaps col-

lege life at the turn of the twentieth century
was the last survival in America of the faith-
in-energy and confidence-in-the-future of the
pioneer experience in America. We youngsters
broke loose from the stabilities of our home
towns in order to find independence in the midst
of opportunity, precisely as did the pioneers
from the East to the West. Like them we knew
that same lift of spirit, release of energy, and
inner fear which one finds recorded in many
frontier diaries. Our competitions, like theirs,
were chiefly in brawn and shrewdness, and, like
hunting, fishing, exploring, and even tree-cut-
ting, were essentially fun, though we, by choice,
and they, by necessity, made work of them.
The horizon of our ambitions, too, was distant
and vague, with miles ahead in which to try
something new if one failed at first. And college, like the frontier, was a young man's
world, where no one got tired, and no energies
were saved for tomorrow. The quick emotions
of the pioneer were ours also, and his boastful-
ness, and his ignorance of subtleties in human
relationships, and his quite unjustified confidence in his self-sufficiency. From his grossness,
his frequent degeneracy, his savagery and shift-

lessness, we were saved by our economic security and civilized environment, though not from his frequent dishonesty. But we did not escape his maladjustment to the realities of a rapidly changing civilization. For even as many a pioneer became a restless vagabond seeking only change all his life, so many a student of my day has stayed mentally an undergraduate ever since.

But most of all in its virtues and in its ideals, did this college life resemble pioneering. The pioneers and the undergraduates were both expecting to get rich, but that was ultimate. The immediate goal was to be regarded as a success by your friends. Ordinary students might be satisfied with a release of energy, but the leaders of the college community wished to be known as the big men, the bad men, the bosses of the neighborhood. Strength, pluck, good nature, square-dealing among friends, shrewd trickiness with enemies, won prestige in both lives. Our emotional range was narrower, for while they dragged their women with them, there were no women in our society except the prostitutes, who were hearty barbarians like ourselves, giving and expecting nothing but a temporary companionship. But if we had no real hardships, we made our lives often incredibly hard, so that it used to be said that a prominent undergraduate was as busy as the President, racing from training table to field, from field to classroom, from classroom to fraternity conference. The youngsters who "heeled" the daily college paper, which was one of the surest roads to social success, slept never more than four hours a night, wore out a bicycle a month, and were rusticated or sent to the infirmary by dozens. They were, ostensibly, learning journalism, but very few of them ever became journalists; they were said to be training themselves for success in after life, a vague future success, like the pioneer's dream (not often realized) of rich and boundless land all his own. Yet in that moment of college time, actually they were playing the game because it was strenuous, and successful strenuosity was certain of recognition by your fellows. It was power in themselves and credit for that power which they sought, not power over others—that desire came later. And so it was with the pioneers also.

I suppose this is where our college generation in its maturity gets its confidence that ability plus hard work can always win the game. For many it has been an illusion. Probably it had become an illusion in America before we entered college. Yet the faith was there, and faith often upsets circumstance. It will take more than the economic shifts of the thirties to convince us that there is any probable set-up of forces that we cannot, if we will, overcome. In our background we have the fact of happiness, relative for most, absolute for some, and that is of immense psychological importance. We have the experience of successful co-operation in our own self-interest. We have the pioneer's training in self-dependence, his sense of room at the top, and his certainty that work can get him there. The proletariat of the United States has had no such experience; the white-collar class of the bourgeoisie that did not go to college, have had no such experience, and if they have the faith, it has already been proved an illusion. It seemed no illusion to us in our fortunate time, which is one reason why foreigners prophesy so badly about the future of the United States. Seeing our economic disorder, they expect leadership from new classes that have no confidence, and as yet no hope except to be themselves of a dominant class. They do not understand that will is strongest among the graduates of the college life.

Our handicap was the lack of a real education. For we never learned what were the possible goals of strenuosity and the limitations of confidence, nor how to apply our energies to a co-operative endeavor which was not a kind of a game, to be won by our side. We were prepared to create a trust or organize a war, not to control the one for human uses and to stop the other before it began. Only the Sumners, and their like, told us what it was all about in terms that penetrated our busy brains. The rest of the adult thinking in our college community was as narrow as our own, even if deeper and truer.

I had a classmate whose father had been governor and was then chief justice of a state. He had been bred in the usual preparatory school routine and was as deep as any of us in the excitements of college life, and rather more irresponsible. But perhaps because he had lived in a home where ideas and their application to the conduct of society had been in daily discussion, he had acquired the rare quality of liking to think. At midnight, when the perennial topics of teams, senior societies, or the amorous or drunken exploits of Student A and Student B, had begun to stale like the pipe smoke, his skeptical spirit would often rise above the trivial, and he would begin to talk in a monologue addressed more to himself than to us. There were ideas afloat, it seemed, which Professor So-and-So had evidently heard of, but bungled in his morning lecture, and these ideas were important to young fellows like us. It was possible that sociology and economics weren't taken seriously enough by the students;—that a lot of the things being taught us, except physics (here we all spat), had stuff in them we ought to think about. Suppose it were true that while we were pretending to be loafers and drunkards the real thing was getting away from us! In Oxford and Cambridge and Paris and Berlin (he had read) there were plenty of dubs and bluffers, yet men like ourselves, who might be ignorant as hell but weren't exactly stupid, got as excited about ideas as over their football games when they had any. He had heard that discussion spread from the good minds on the faculty through the student body; that men came out of those universities ready to stir up a rumpus in the world, ahead of the game, not behind it. Men were graduated there not into law or the soap business, but into radicalism or imperialism, all hot with some new philosophy. They went home interested in thinking, which certainly never happened to a chairwarmer at Heublein's café, or a heeler of the football team, or the last man to be tapped for a senior society, provided that was all he did in college. What was the matter with us? Had we no *Weltanschauung* (or this is what he would have said, if he had not been so rotten in German), no sense of responsibility for a country that was after all not just a place where you looked for a job?

We would shift uncomfortably, making feeble rejoinders, which grew more confident as we sketched the outline of yesterday's economics recitation (which we knew he had flunked), asking what Ricardo meant in our young lives, until the breezes blew once more from our real interests, and the talk lifted into the untroubled blue of college gossip.

I did some thinking myself in those days, not much, for like most of my college generation, my moods were either intensely romantic or very practical, neither good for thinking. I got far enough with my self-scrutiny to begin to read a little on my own, but never to a clear realization of why abstract thinking was unfashionable in the college community.

It is clear enough now. We resisted the intrusion of abstract ideas because our skin was full to bursting of our own affairs and our minds hot with our own enthusiasms. Most of us (certainly the most influential among us) were still school boys whose contacts with the outside world, if any, had been with the new expansionist United States, competitive, unscrupulous, intensely individualistic, grandiose in economic plans, yet with no vision beyond construction, production, accumulation. In my own time and class in college, one could have ticked off the new trusts by the sons of their beneficiaries—oil, steel, lumber,—and the great railroads by their heirs. Of course we never thought that way, except shrewd managers of fraternities looking for new buildings. Yet it was true that our college was a cross-section of American wealth and a residuary legatee of economic leadership.

Our tendency was therefore to make the college into another and better competitive Amer-

ica.   We did not want to think about it, we
wanted to be it.   In the nineteen thirties we
have been taught to estimate that expansionist
age in terms of great forces wielded by builders,
wreckers, pirates, who were quite unconscious
that they were working for anything but their
own wealth and power.   We of the college were
quite innocent of such speculations, and thought
of the magnates, when we thought of them at
all, only as men who had made good.   But of
the fierce competitions in which they were the
captains and the kings we were of course not
unaware, being acutely conscious that success in
our collegiate world would seat us on the great
American band wagon.   More of this later,
when I get to the nature of our real education.
Hence our interests, our motives, our activities,
which seem so adolescent to the realistic youth
of today, were all subtly related to the competitive energies running loose in the American scene.
We belonged by birth and breeding to the dominant party of action in America, not to the re-
cessive and unheard opposition of those who still
speculated upon how life ought to be lived.
Therefore in college, if we thought at all, it was
upon how to get on, not upon the results of get-

ting there, and we were graduated by thousands ready to join the builders and the wreckers of the country, but almost unaware that architects were needed. The interpenetration from science, scholarship, philosophy which operated in other educational systems seldom took place, because there was no room in our minds for ideas so foreign to our interests. This was why in my room that night we stumbled and faltered, trying to find arguments to justify our passionate interest in a college life which, after all, was often trivial, and sometimes childish, and yet which couldn't be shrugged off in a debate without making us feel somehow or another unAmerican.

We were right. Anything else for us just then would have been unAmerican—which is not to compliment America. And indeed the last twenty years have proved that there was more vitality in this college life we pursued so devotedly than in the curriculum which the "grinds" admired. The graduates of college life have used a great orchestra to make cheap music; but the best the "grinds" could do was to play second fiddle.

Certainly this college experience was a life, and hence, since we were young, a vital education. In every later period of my own experience I have lived several lives at once—in my business, in my home, in my thinking, and in my emotional experiences. But in the heyday of the turn of the college century, for most of us everything was concentrated in an intense and isolated unity. In the classroom, it is true, we could sit and sit while ideas about evolution or Shakespeare dropped upon us like the gentle rain from heaven, which seeped in or evaporated according to our mental temperatures. But there was no such lassitude in college life. The environment was too powerful. It burnt up old social distinctions and made new ones. It shriveled one set of illusions and created another much more powerful. In that rough and tumble of athletics, social drinking, and doing something for the old college, all the classes of America except the socially impossible and the intellectually prim were thoroughly mingled. Veils of glamour in older countries have protected rank and wealth—especially in those college aristocracies nearest to our own, Oxford and Cambridge. Not so with us. They were stripped away from our young plutocrats. After the sons and heirs who might have formed an American aristocracy of wealth and privilege had been shuffled in the college competitions with the shrewd children of parvenus and the good baseball players whose fathers were Irish policemen, cards were redealt in new social categories. Though John Brown might be the son of the president of the United Steel Corporation, in college he was known as left guard on the football team, or a hustler for the Y. M. C. A. who had made a senior society. Or if he had made it on steel only (which was not improbable) his prestige sank to plus zero before the end of senior year. We knew him too well to take him seriously as one who should rank above us because he was rich. In college we were surprisingly humble in the presence of the Big Men, the class leaders, who so often later proved to have been Stuffed Shirts, precocious adolescents with no staying power; yet at least they had made their own greatness, did not bring it with them unless from successes in preparatory school. But we were not impressed by the Great Names of plutocracy—by Vanderbilts, Astors, Rockefellers as such—since we saw them at first hand. And thus, with our realistic experience in the qualified democracy of the colleges died the possibility of

adding to the economic privileges of the very rich the respect given elsewhere to rank. It is thanks to the American college that smart-set society in America has seemed important only to the lower middle class. Although economically illiterate in theory, in practice we were prepared in advance for a true estimate of the calibre of our economic masters and the society they supported.

But this talk of "economic masters" belongs to the thirties. In the nineties and first nineteen hundreds, this fiercely competitive college life was romantic, not realistic to those that lived it. It is hard to recall to a colder age the deep inferiorities, burning frustrations, and glowing confidences of those few years that seemed to us so long. I can still shiver with humiliation over slights remembered for thirty odd years, and warm at the memory of unforgettable mirth. Romance, to be valid, must be intensely real, and stand up through space and time against the tests of disillusionment. That was true, is true, for the college life of my college generation.

It was not a wine, that romance, which could be kept for others. There was too much *fin de siècle* in it. You had to drink it while you and the century were young. It is difficult to look with a serious eye upon the youngsters of my day as they appear in the old photographs. I see my classmates strolling to recitation, or draped in a row on a fence—chubby-faced boys dressed in knee-tight knickerbockers of black and white check, with natty little jockey caps, also checked, or with derbies cocked rakishly over ties which I remember to have been scarlet. Or it is the summer of 1899, and we are wearing tiny straw hats with negligible brims, and voluminous white ducks under neat little coats whose tails scarcely cover our waistbands. Yet under these comic collegiate clothes the hearts of even the careerists and the drunkards beat with romance, and could be stirred to a passion of loyalty at a hint that our college (by which was meant our college life) was not the best in the world.

We were barbarians, but we were romantic barbarians, and so adapted our rowdy manners very quickly to the new Tudor Gothic which was just beginning to step back the American campus into an imitation middle ages. In my day at Yale the active leaders of college life lived in the barn-like rooms of the Colonial Lyceum.

That was the heart of the college. But already
its romantic soul had found expression in Gothic
dormitories in whose courtyards I walked often
by moonlight to enjoy a setting that shed distinction upon our loyalties. The Gothic walls
seemed to shut off our college competitions from
the cruder world outside us, and fostered the
illusion of an American Utopia. Others less impressionable than I, and more powerful, were
infected with a like romance and poured out
millions later into brick and stone antiquarianism to realize their ideal.

But in its beginnings this romanticism was
certainly a phase of the *fin de siècle*. It set us
youngsters who were literary to editing chap
books, writing ballads, and constructing smart
short stories where the quip was everything and
the content nothing. We reacted from our
strenuous materialism into pose and affectation
as the college builders reacted from the utilitarianism of the eighties into sham parapet and
needless arch. They went in for Gothic, and we
for the Yellow Book. We were cured quickly
by the realism of the tens and twenties, and by
the war. Their delusion still persists.

I went to a reunion of my class a year or so

ago in company with old friends who had been
with me in senior year. Together we searched
out the house in which we had lived off campus,
which not being a college dormitory had survived the boom days of the twenties when most
of the buildings so well remembered had been
scrapped to make place for Gothic grandeur.
Climbing familiar stairs we found the room in
which we had spent so many happy hours. It
was a grimy sordid mess of broken furniture,
peeling walls, and rotting window seat, in which
some Jewish old clothes man had found a home.
Remembering the golden excitements of those
days, and seeing on the window sills initials
carved of men long dead, the appropriate tears
of sentiment should have flowed—for there had
been nothing quite like those hours since, or
could be for us, or would be in our unconfident
times again. But I was not too much moved to
note how commonplace after all was the room,
the ornaments of the fireplace which we had built
how trivial, how garish the figures of the wall
paper which we had thought so beautiful, the
whole with its memories now actualized on the
very spot so like an old stage set outmoded and
decayed. When the vitality of youth had run

out of that room there was nothing considerable left.

And this seems to be the truth about our college life. It was powerful for us, but the staying power of Puritanism, for example, the intellectual fabric of a church, the elements of a culture, were not in it. It was like a vigorous kick of a football, too high, too aimless, into a drift of adverse winds. Yet that kick, if it was not, like the shot at Concord Bridge, heard round the world, was felt throughout America. Behind it was the college spirit—naive intellectually but emotionally vigorous, the still youthful soul of the last great age of romantic American individualism.

CHAPTER III

Education: Common and Preferred

WHEN we had been in college two or three years, and after the college town, the campus, the Green, the crowded pavements of the city streets, were tracked with our familiar comings and goings, the glamour still had gold in it. Indeed to this day I pass on Fifth Avenue or Piccadilly a man of my own age whose name I do not know, yet whose face faintly stirs the memory of excitement and romance—and know him to be one of my college world of the turn of the century, a fellow traveller with me who must remember, as I remember, the confident self-sufficiency of that island in time. He too was in our fancied Arcady, and yet I knew him only by sight as we sat at nearby tables at Mory's or rubbed elbows in the campus crowd.

That Arcady was intensely American. Its only resemblance to the Greek pastoral romance was our naive certainty that we were living in a golden age, and perhaps our absorption in our own affairs. College life for us was at least 90% of our felt experience, and therefore 90% of the college as we knew it. Thus it became, as I have said, our real education, for every hard-lived life is an education, and no education educates unless it is lived.

But that was not the opinion of the faculty, or even of the college town and our parents. The official idea of education differed sharply from ours and was formulated, whereas ours was instinctive. We had the personnel, but the faculty controlled the tenure of residence, so that a conflict was inevitable, and this conflict created one of those situations that make real history, the kind that until twenty or thirty years or a century later never gets into books.

The American college of those days was certainly one of the most delightful escapes for youths restless in cramped environments, yet it was also one of the most irrational and confusing educational institutions the world has ever seen. Its façade had little relation to its interior, its back door was very much more important than its front. Raw boys were dipped into college life, to emerge, after four years of strenuous idleness, mature, self-sufficient, and confident that they were educated. This was the experience to which father really referred, whether he realized it or not, when he would say proudly, "Yes, our boy is going to college."

But our college was also a *collegium,* a fellowship of scholars and of teachers with their pupils, devoted to disciplining and liberalizing the youthful mind by doses of an enforced curriculum. This was the college of the catalogue, about which essays upon education were written. With this *collegium* we students had a compulsory acquaintance, which varied from the bum's consciousness of a policeman just around the corner, to an amicable arrangement by which so much acquired knowledge should be paid back in small change into the dean's office, in return for an adequate minimum of marks,

This college seldom educated us, but it did temper the excesses and sweeten the content of our real, our preferred education, in college life, and it sowed in our inattentive minds seeds of ideas which often sprouted later. Also it gave us frames of reference which became useful in after life, and sometimes, but not always, taught us how to read.

And there was a third aspect of this college of the catalogue to which I, as a junior, scorching on my bicycle from a class in English to a student meeting, was almost oblivious, but which must be mentioned here. Around the college had grown up in the latter nineteenth century a haphazard, ill-balanced collection of professional schools, attended by hard-working meagre creatures with the fun drained out of them, who were looked upon with suspicion by the undergraduates, since few of them had been graduated from our college. These schools plus ourselves made up the university, a circus in which the college was the main ring, with law, theology, medicine, and graduate studies in science or the humanities, for side-shows. The central current of American life, as it was then, flowed through the college, carrying with it the rich spoils of American prosperity, and also respect and affection for this unique institution, which was called, by a strange misapprehension of its strenuous temperament, *alma mater*. The university, feeding upon this life stream, eventually grew great upon its nourishment, but it was in my day a parasite sucking for its own excellent purposes the blood of the college, or more accurately, of that college life which engendered the loyalty of gift-giving alumni. At the moment when the glamorous college life which dominated us and the college was most vigorous, while we sat at Heublein's drinking our beer and assessing the future in terms of the football team, the leaders of American education were planning to make the sprawling university into a vast system of professional training which now begins to dominate both the college and America.

Not so in 1900, when it was still the college that gave America the kind of education it wanted, and conferred the only class distinction that counted everywhere. Could an M. A. or a Ph. D. or an LL. B. or an M. D. make a youth into a Yale or a Harvard man? Never! Only the bachelor's degree with four years of college life behind it gave that almost sacred consecration. No one else had been baptized and confirmed in the college spirit, converted and changed to the type of college man supposedly bred only in the Yard or on the Campus. Of education in research and for the comprehension and reconstruction of society I shall have something to say later. Higher education, as the nineties and the early nineteen hundreds thought

of it, was quite different—it was the education
of college life, which was something so specific,
so highly charged with emotion, so powerful in
its influences upon behavior, that it may be said
to have been 100% efficient at a time when higher
education in the sense common to all the ages had
touched only here and there American habits of
thought. Whatever the science or the scholarship of these professional schools suburban to the
campus (and it was considerable), it was the
college that educated the class that was to rule
the country for the next generation, so that in
any discussion of education in the early twentieth century it is essential not to overlook this
education by college life. There was, however,
the other kind also, common and commonplace
to all of us, but not preferred.

I went to college at a time when (fortunately
for an observer) an old curriculum was still tot-
tering like a rotted house about to fall and in
parts already fallen. Before my day college education had been disciplinary. The curriculum
was a beautiful unity; neat, harmonious, and
inspiring confidence because so many generations
had worked out the rules for extracting the
maximum of mental discipline from the age-

tested subjects of which it was composed. It consisted of the classics, long since emptied of the noble excitements of the Renaissance, but efficiently organized into exercises in grammar and bilinguality; of mathematics; of rhetoric; and of some philosophy, literature, and history;—all taught by men who believed in hard work upon hard subjects as the first of the intellectual virtues. It was a training rather than an education, yet it had the merit of all systems carried through to a logical conclusion. The professors of that day were taskmasters and looked their part. Some of them still survived in our expansive period, bearded men, a little dusty, whose clothes and faces were as emphatically different from the world's as were the old-time clergymen's. Men sure of themselves, severe, arid, uncompromising, uninventive, uninterested in the constantly new thing which we call life, yet often unexpectedly wise and serene. Or so they seemed in the decay of the age of discipline.

For of course it had to decay, since its discipline was based upon a superstitious belief in the exclusive validity of an inherited learning. By our time not even the professors really believed in the efficacy of the old curriculum. They had faith in their own subjects still, but were patently aware that few agreed with them. How many classrooms do I remember where instruction consisted in a calling up of one man after another to translate from a heavily cribbed text of Latin, Greek, or French! How many an English recitation where in sleepy routine the questions went round:—"What does our author say about Lucifer's ambitions?—Who was Ben Jonson and what were his relations to Shakespeare?" Never in business, in law, even in religion, has there been more sham, bunk, and perfunctoriness than in the common education of the American college in that easy-going time. It seemed to me incredible that a mature and civilized person, who in private life had an impeccable character and often geniality and charm, should be willing to earn a living (and usually a meagre living) by asking trivial questions day after day of young men who had either memorized the answers as the easiest way of getting on with college life and their real education, or constructed a system of bluff so transparent that only a defeatist who did not believe in education would have stood for it. I understand more now of the exigencies of life and the conditions upon which a scholar was permitted to be an intellectual in those days. Even so I wonder when I think of men I know who have persisted in this rigamarole for thirty years.

The younger members of the faculty were in still graver difficulties, as I soon discovered when after graduation I stayed on in my *alma mater*. If they belonged to the college, they held their heads much higher than teachers assigned to the tribes without the law—to postgraduates, medical students, and such rabble. And why? Because they were close to the throb of life on the campus, where America was really in the making, because they were in power over youngsters who so obviously were representative of the ruling class of the roaring industrial world outside, which in itself they dreaded or disliked. Their training and their reason taught them that they must fight the materialism spilling over into the campus from this American energy on the loose, or be downed by it. Yet they knew that they could never do it with the old curriculum, which was as external to the real existence of the undergraduate as his clothes to his body. They were on a hot spot, and the inconsistency of their conduct (admiring the undergraduate, while hat-ing his ideas) did not help to make effective the kind of education they were hired to distribute. The tension was good for their personalities, which often became memorable, but effectually broke up what confidence still existed in the old discipline.

That disciplinary education had been devised for a small class, largely professional or aristocratic. It had given to the lawyer not merely the Latin he needed, but a training in dialectics, which may have been a factor in keeping his profession twenty years behind the other departments of social service. It gave to the non-professional man that look into a heart of another culture which broadened him for life; and it could do this because there were no distractions of college life or new knowledge to interfere with the slow unwrapping of the grammatical husk from the rich meat of the classics. It had the merit of all incantations when the neophytes believe in their efficiency.

But the nineteen hundreds of which I write was a new world in which science was already dominant; it was a prosperous world in America where the luxury of a class education was open to thousands; it was a world conscious of immense vitality, re-creating the behavior of societies, breaking up old orders of life. Mathematics and Virgil, Kant, rhetoric, and ancient history, were no longer enough. Even to undergraduates new subjects were being taught by scores, though usually by the old methods. Youth answered questions about physics and zoölogy instead of about grammar and the genealogies of the Bible. Evolution was being lectured upon. Sociology and economics were under way. Only government lagged, for we Americans still felt that the founding fathers had handed down from Sinai all we needed to know about government. The conventional curriculum was no longer a summary of the intellectual experience of the race.

It became unhappily a digest of examinable subjects about which concrete questions could be answered after due memorizing, and to which other subjects could be added, such as psychology, as soon as they could be made examinable. Although the personality of great teachers might break through, although there were exceptions in new methods, that was the deadly daily round of formal college education which took the place of the old discipline. And that was how I was taught at the beginning of the century, and how I began to teach a little later after careful instruction in the routine of implanting, and then extracting, the facts which my classes were supposed to regurgitate from their texts and textbooks, turning literature into a selection of things said by an author, language into a set of declensions and conjugations, and writing into an exercise in spelling, grammar, and the making of a plan for composing what concerned no one, least of all the writer.

If this had been all to college education in those days, there would have been no alumni turning back to *alma mater*, and certainly no book, but only a dirge, to write about the American college. It was, of course, not the real college education at all. That was a life, a powerful, conditioning life, from which only the "grinds" and rare sophisticates escaped without a moulding of character and intellect, and a complete reshaping of behavior.

Why did they go to college, those thousands upon mounting thousands that crowded into the campuses in those decades? Entrance examinations were stiffened to hold them back (a boon to tutoring schools), subjects which, like Greek,

the schools refused to teach, were kept in the requirements in the hope of barring the gate. Yet
still they came until in many an institution all
obstacles were swept away and the prosperous multitude was greeted with a triumphant
despair.

They came for the best of reasons. They
swarmed from the drab experience of small town
or commercial city, direct or via the boarding-
schools, because they had heard of college life,
where instead of the monotony of school discipline or the bourgeois experience which had
succeeded their confident childhood, there was
singing, cheering, drinking, and the keenest competition for honor and prestige, a life rich in the
motives which were being stifled in the struggle
for power in the adult world outside. They
desired romance, they sought distinction, and
were not unwilling to spend some bookish labor
in order to win the opportunities of a class that
called itself educated.

These were the naives, and perhaps by far the
largest number of aspirants. The shrewder and
less romantic shared some of these anticipations
but mingled with them ambitions much more
realistic. They had learned in the preparatory

schools that the college world was a career as well as a Utopia; and furthermore, a career where the sharp and energetic might overcome handicaps of birth, poverty, or even of character. They knew that this college boasted of its democracy, which actually was no social democracy at all, since class lines (once drawn) were tighter than in the outside world. They knew well that it was a democracy of opportunity. In the home town you were either born into the right group, and, if your family kept its money, stayed there; or, with greater or less difficulty, depending upon where you lived, forced yourself into society and its privileges by the sheer power of money. Self-made riches came hard. But in college life there were other stairways that led to security. Money counted, social standing outside counted, yet the son of a shopkeeper could get as far on athletic prowess as the gilded child of privilege on his family momentum. Good looks counted also, more, I should say in the men's than in the women's colleges; and so did good clothes if worn in the collegiate manner which required the slovenly use of expensive and well-cut garments. Wit, and the gift of being amusing, especially when tight, were very helpful; and so was political sagacity. And, as I have said, there were routes upward for boys who could write what the college magazine wanted, or make the kind of music that undergraduates liked; and a broad path, much trodden in my day, for the energetically pious who could organize religion, and sell God to the right kind of undergraduate. They were sure of a senior society. It was to be twenty years before Dr. Buchman would realize the exceeding potency of a blend of religious craving with social fastidiousness, and create the Oxford Movement out of his experience with undergraduates.

These shrewd and realistic students who went to college as careerists, were well aware that this college climbing led to much more than a college success. From a commonplace family in a commonplace town, with no prospect ahead but a grind of money-making and association with other stuffy nobodies, the youngster whose parents had invested in a college education, might hope to pass by his own native abilities into the brave, translunary world of great cities and the gilded corridors of their privileged sets. For if he could once place himself in the right college group, his own would take care of him, provided

[71]

that he did not too egregiously disappoint them in his later career.   From henceforth he would be not Jones of Columbus, but Jones of "Bones" or some other tight-ringed fraternity.   Thanks to his ability to catch a ball, or to organize, or to be friendly, or to drink like a gentleman, or even to capitalize his charm, he was tapped as of the elect at age 20 or 21, and had precisely that advantage (and no more) which rank and privilege still gave in the Old World.   If there was a good job in a brokerage firm he would get it, because of his connections.   If there was a right club where he was going, he could join it.   And all this he himself could win, unaided by the power of money or the accident of social position, and find himself, after a few brief years of struggle, companioned with the sons of plutocrats and the aristocracy.   It is no wonder that college life in these nineties and early nineteen hundreds was for many an intoxicating dream.

This life was clearly an education.   Its code was definite and hard.   Study must not be taken too seriously, but only a fool would fail to pay the lip service to intellectual endeavor required by the authorities.   Yet it did not have to be lip service only, since the undergraduates in the education they preferred had worked out a compromise with formal study very much like the tacit agreement to go to church without being religious which their elders had made with the church. These students were after all to be known as college men, and so they intended to become acquainted, if not familiar, with the best that was being thought and said, able at will to speak of the things of the mind without letting them get in the way of interested action. One could tell a college graduate in those days by his lighter touch upon the problems of making a living—he knew that man does not live by bread alone, yet proposed to get his bread and get it easily.

This code also recognized and required competition as the test of life. There was no fiercer competition in the business world than the undergraduate competition for social rewards. Beside its strenuosities the pursuit of marks or even of scholarship glowed dimly. And this competition was involved in that curious complex of juvenile idealism already described which made the unremitting labors of a crew manager or football captain seem a patriotic service, so that the man who had been most energetic and successful in athletics or college politics was invariably said to have done the most for his college, as indeed he had if by college one means the vital social organism to which he really belonged and not the intellectual institution in which he spent his spare time. Indeed that fervor of public service which had animated the early Republic, especially in the South, and which had by now been submerged in a fever of individualistic industrialism, still persisted in the colleges in this adolescent form. And like all idealisms, however juvenile, it sweetened the self-interest of competitors who so evidently and consciously were feathering their own nests. This code of competition in, but also very definitely for, the group brought with it other virtues, such as loyalty, tenacity, generosity, courage, and a willingness to co-operate, which made the college career, so trivial in its immediate objectives, so irrelevant to the purposes of scholarship, nobler, or at least less selfish and sordid, than the power-seeking society for which it was obviously a preparation. It did not, I fear, make it more honest.

In short, college life, which was so often criticized or laughed at, did educate for adult life afterward, and specifically for American life in what was its most typical if not its most admirable aspect. It inculcated ideals that were viable in America as it was then, and these ideals were adaptations of general idealism (even of Christianity) to the needs of an industrialized, get-rich-quick country. It educated specifically for the harsh competitions of capitalism, for the successful and often unscrupulous pursuit by the individual of power for himself, for class superiority, and for a success measured by the secure possession of the fruits of prosperity. I do not see how a better education could have been contrived for a youth that wanted the wealth, the position, the individual power that was being worshipped just then in America,—and wanted to get them quickly, easily, and with no public dishonesty. If, indeed, without straining the term to the breaking-point, you can call a training for a career of this sort a true education!

Nevertheless, this education by college life was at least designed to make the youth a little more civilized than those who missed it. It began the shattering of that idea of dollar supremacy which had shocked Europeans from the beginnings of the American experiment. Of all the talents use-

ful for success in the college community the gift
of money-making was least esteemed. This was
attributable only in part to the obvious fact that
most of us had money from our parents, though
never enough of it. Boys without resources,
who worked their way through college, were respected for their pluck and sometimes reached
social eminence, but it was not their skill in
money-making that got them there. Our society
was like the nonprofit-making orders of the
Middle Ages. It was a community in which
what you did, not what you got, earned rewards
that were never financial, although they might
lead to financial security afterwards. The boy
who had gone through this college life was well
aware of the value of wealth and usually determined to have his share of it, yet he also knew by
intimate experience of the value of other sources
of prestige. He would never judge the successful
clergyman, doctor, or even professor by his income solely. He had become tolerant of any
kind of success.

Of course this shrewd blend of a romantic and
a practical education was quite incompatible
with the disinterested search for truth for which
colleges, among other purposes, were supposed

to be founded.   We were not looking for truth,
—we were seeking either a romantic illusion, or
material success, which often proved later to be
also an illusion.   If we were by nature idealists,
and many were in that twilight of the Age of
Confidence, we turned our backs on the unlovely
but immensely vital America outside, took refuge in the Gothic of our imitation monastery,
and extracted a brand of happiness by becoming
true products of the mauve decade.   And if we
were not idealists, if we were parvenus on the
make, or shrewd youngsters aware that college
life was a Christmas tree for the *fortunati* who
picked the right envelopes from the branches,
why then it was no great surprise to us to learn
that the idols of college worship were much the
same as the idols of the market place, with a different coat of paint.

A dose of illusion is good for youth, and so is
a shot of romance, and certainly no sociologist
could fail to admire the perfect adaptation of
our preferred education to the *mores* of the
American life we were about to enter.   The irony
lay in a confusion of values and purposes.   It is
surely the duty of an educational institution to
prepare for a change in *mores,* since *mores* are

always in process of changing.   But our college, with the university then gathering round it, carried too much earthy ballast ever to lift far above the society that supported it.   The college could make a class set apart by special behavior, but it could not impregnate that class with superior ideas.   College life was so vital in itself and so formative that ideas, the search for truth, scholarship, and the forecasts and interpretations of the intellect in general, were inevitably mere by-products of an institution whose service was to teach competition and the public-school code. Even professors and presidents believed that then, no matter what their mouths said.   College life was the heart of the educational machine. Research became possible because alumni of the college paid the heavy expenses of an institution which they had moulded and continued to mould to their own desires, but in whose ample margins there was room and support for the reflective, the analytical, the creative mind, which could get little if any sustenance elsewhere in a bustling, money-making country.   The scholar could collect books into a great library, build and use laboratories, work, think, and discuss, provided that he did not get in the way of the social-educational program of college life, provided usually that he gave either the perfunctory end of his teaching time to the undergraduate, or helped to camouflage the incongruities of the hybrid institution he served by the dignity of his name in the international world of scholarship. What shrieks rent the heavens when, at the end of the period of which I write, money that might have been had for the college proper began to flow into medical, law, and graduate schools! With what enormous satisfaction did the alumni welcome the final triumph of the Gothic scheme which at frightful expense (far greater than any costs of pure education) transformed the ugly college of the nineties into a new Oxford, equipped not like the original for monastic students, but with every appurtenance of the life of the very rich, and housed in the ornate plush-in-stone of the late Middle Ages which gave a striking effect of class exclusiveness. I write not entirely in sorrow, for the college was vital, it was happy, it deserved to be dressed in fine linen and set upon a throne. And the buildings, even the most pretentious, and certainly the reconstructions of Colonial architecture which many a college has preferred to Tudor Gothic, are much superior to

Main Street. And yet what possibilities of a neurosis lay in this strange set of compromises involving education, romance, and materialism! I doubt whether values were ever more completely mixed, muddled, and concealed than in the battle (if you can call it that) between our perfunctory and our preferred education.

CHAPTER IV

The Faculty

IN THE years of which I have just written, and particularly in the first decade of the new century, they were trying in our college to combine various incompatibles, and if some of the consequences were lamentable it was an exciting experiment for students and faculty alike. When the college began we Americans had been still English by one remove, with the strong imitativeness of Colonials, and so naturally we had begun (and were still trying) to adapt to American conditions the morale, the atmosphere, and the objectives of the English public school. But our boys when they were allowed to leave home were already approaching college age so that this public-school tradition was applied by us to the four years of college. Colonial also was our admiration for the aristocratic English Utopias of Oxford and Cambridge. We borrowed their curriculum and imitated their exclusiveness, but gave it a democratic slant by making college life itself a social distinction, which would be useful in the competitive system, intensely bourgeois, of a rapidly industrializing America. And these incongruities the presidents and faculties of my day proposed to blend with the idea of a university. No wonder that a young instructor on the faculty in, say, 1905, could look upon this unheard of combination of sporting resort, beer garden, political convention, laboratory, and factory for research with a mind as confused as a Spanish omelet.

I became a young instructor in the early nineteen hundreds—and can testify to the curious psychological state of a college faculty that had to oversee a dual education in which college life and the college curriculum pretended each to be unaware of the other's existence, except when they met head on in a collision over the marking system. It was then that I began to reinterpret my undergraduate experience with education in terms of an adult whose business it was to teach.

The first-rate scholar—and there were always a few of them—did his job regardless of the competition with college life. I remember at Yale of my day, Gibbs, the creator of the mathematical technique upon which much of modern physics and its stupendous practical achievement is based. Shy, remote, a lean, dim figure on the streets, not even his closest colleagues guessed that a generation later his name would be used to persuade the world that we were an institution primarily devoted to learning.

Mathematicians were fortunate; it was easy for them to escape the romantic materialism which college life had imposed upon college education. But if the great scholar was also a powerful lecturer on subjects less abstract, his place in our world was that of *avocatus diaboli*. He was like the rebel leader of a band of guerrillas hovering on the flank of our complacent army, his onslaughts too vigorous to be ignored, yet too fleeting to threaten the impregnable smugness of our college life and thought. Only later did one discover the uncomfortable idea, the tiny realization, stuck like a chance arrow in the mind to poison self-assurance. Such a man in our day was William Graham Sumner.

The second-rate scholar or teacher was less fortunate. His literature, his history, or his science could make little headway against the hot

[83]

tides of the real college education, which was college life. In self-defense he fell back upon the marking system, which, like a dam in a sandy river, was always being built higher to check the tricky currents that invariably formed new channels beside or beneath it. See him, mark book in hand, distributing morning questions to an inattentive class, hoping that if it could not be made to drink of his knowledge, it could at least be frightened into going through the motions. Somewhat pathetically he stands upon his dignity, suppresses titters, talks for his own ear, and too often secretes a bilious contempt for his barbarians which he will later purge by hard work on his edition of the Song of Roland (a poem about barbarians) or his paper on the ablatives in Suetonius. And if the fruits of his scholarship became arid until dryness itself began to seem a virtue, any psychologist could tell you that this was an inevitable result of contacts with the disinterest or disdain of an outer world that for him was represented by the undergraduates. However, I must leave the neuroses of teaching for another chapter where they may be discussed with more insight and kindliness. In this account of what the college did to its faculty, there is no room for the special cases that sometimes seemed to justify the whole incongruous compromise.

The puzzled instructor might see the muddle he was in, and squirm there ineffectually. Older men reacted more definitely, and one result was to make this college era the age of personalities in American teaching. The weak submitted to the double standards which governed them; the strong rebelled with all the strength of their temperaments. They could not remake their environment, yet individually, and often against carping criticism, they set out to bring back vitality into what the catalogue called education. Discipline was failing, research and the analysis of ideas were too remote from undergraduate interests and perhaps from their own,—so they substituted enthusiasm. We distrust enthusiasm now, and most of all it is distrusted by the new type of clear-headed, skeptical student. It was a blessing then, which gave to my generation what little feeling for science and the humanities we possess.

The undergraduate of those days was intellectually a primitive, whose thoughts were busy with athletics, pleasure, and social ambition.

Emotionally he was more mature. The vitality of college life had made him vital. He was aroused, eager, sensitive, as is readily proved by the vividness with which men of my age remember the least details of their four years of college experience. And hence, when a new type of professor came striding into the dead classrooms, with a quip on his tongue, and a sudden lifting of dull, perfunctory subjects of instruction into interest, beauty, or excitement, his students responded with a stir of the intellectual being. It is true that history might be interpreted for them in terms of the football season, Dante translated into the jargon of the Y. M. C. A., or Shakespeare and Pope denatured into nineteenth century optimism. Yet the gap was often bridged between past and present, and wires strung across over which emotion could travel, until a society that did not resemble New York or Skowhegan, Maine, became a vague reality to youthful minds, while a sense of the imagination as a new major sport grew and never contracted again into the narrowness of our old education.

Thinking was not much helped by this contagious enthusiasm; yet what profitable thinking ever began in the low temperatures of indifference! And these men did not leave us cold. Indeed it was the enthusiasts, whose published works were often thin and sometimes childish, and whose fate it was in a later and more realistic decade to be classed with realtors and revivalists, who best and most easily penetrated the busy hum of college life. They were great men in their way and I look vainly for their compeers now. Preachers not scholars, temperaments rather than characters, with emotions stronger than their minds, they recall to me, with important differences, those passionate Jesuits recruited by Loyola to reinvigorate the sterile church.

But enthusiasts were rare in my time, nor could enthusiasm alone solve a problem that went much deeper than the emotions. The faculty of those days, as a body if not as individuals, had one of the great opportunities of educational history, and muffed it. For so many hours a week, with the lash of dismissal from that pleasant college life as a goad, they had bound to them the pick of the sons of expansionist America, a youth recalcitrant to appeals to the pure intellect, too shrewd to be disciplined, but very sensitive to whatever could be made to seem to be progress. And competition was the breath of their life.

These were no slavish disciples who themselves hoped to enter the academic life, but the next generation of industrial America for whom the capitalists of the predatory age had wrecked, exploited, built. The professors were teaching ten such for one who might become a successor in scholarship. The future political, social, commercial, and industrial leadership of the United States was in college.

Except for a great man here and there—a James, a Sumner, a Wilson, a Wendell, a Gildersleeve—they muffed their opportunity. A revolution in knowledge was under way, science was expanding like the physicist's universe, history was being rewritten, philosophy was in the workshop again, the vitamins of the nineteenth century were passing into the metabolism of the twentieth. Even the humanities were being reinterpreted to suit a new mood. Physicists, biologists, historians, sociologists, economists, were seeing new horizons,—and all with one accord devoted their college energies to making new scientists, new scholars, to carry on after them. They taught physics for physicists, biology for biologists, history for historians. They were not interested in the American youth who was not going to be a specialist, a professor, but only a leader of industrial, commercial, political America. They accepted his indifference to their theories as a natural perversity, and snubbed him or disciplined him according to circumstance. It was as if St. Paul had spent his energies upon raising theologians and let the Gentiles go hang.

Hence, unless the students were of the elect who were to carry on the torch, they were dragged from their heated college competitions and their life of intense companionship to dull classrooms where the object seemed to be to teach them how to answer questions about literature, or to hear scientists try to make zoölogists or geologists out of men predestined for the law or the brokerage business. Such professors flunked the unwilling and hence gained some respect, especially for the more difficult sciences. But of an understanding that this science, this scholarship, was deeply relative to everyone's future, very little did they show. The boys took their medicine as a child takes castor oil, unwillingly, unaware of a reason or of the morrow. And inevitably the students who did go along with the specialists because they had come to college to learn how to be specialists or professors, were suspect to the rest. They seemed a class apart, unAmerican, boys who had no time or inclination for college life, and so were missing what the rest regarded as the most vital education. Well, undergraduate opinion was wrong, as the success of many such has proved; but the faculty was wrong also, as the country-wide failure to teach Americans the control of their own culture equally demonstrates.

I remember, in particular, three of those professors whose job it was while I was still an undergraduate, to compete with our ardent college life. As I think back to their methods and their philosophy of educating us, I see what little chance there was that such men could have crossed the gulf between the two kinds of education. The first of them was living proof that the faculty as well as the students could be perfunctory. He was a round little man who throughout a solid year dictated to us a compendium of world history which I am sure was bad history (all bones, no nerves or blood) and know to have been frightful boredom. At the end we were asked to give it all back to him, which we did, well salted with errors and violent misreadings of our hurried notes. He was incompetent, but apparently good enough as a hurdle between us and a degree.

And one was an old zoölogist well past the age of interest in anything but animal classification. He would drone inaudibly about animal life (which would have fascinated me from less senile lips), while the class stole horrid creatures from his alcohol jars to be dropped later into somebody's plate of soup. Although his own science had left him behind, he was supposed to be good enough for the inferior purpose of educating the Philistine.

To the third, an able economist still in his prime, and an excellent teacher of graduate students, was entrusted the task of explaining economic law to our parcel of young individualists who believed that the philosophy of income and expenditure began and ended with luck and hard work. He opened our eyes to the mechanics of business, but his science, which we were glad to learn was called "dismal," left us quite unaware of any human relationship in finance or the ethics of the distribution of wealth. I learned with amazement some years later that socialism was not a heresy which had expired, like mercantilism, some time in the nineteenth century, and that profit-making was not necessarily an axiom upon which thinking began.

All three of these men misunderstood us, and we them. We were America, young, vigorous, competitive, and very ignorant. They were scholars (or at least two of them were) bred in the idea that their sacred knowledge was a temple set apart from everyday life. We were supposed to forget our concern with living while we studied their theories; but this was not made easier by their concern to separate what they knew from any close reference to contemporary life. For that life seemed confused and barbarous to them. They did not try to understand it, because to do so made their own tasks of abstraction and analysis far more difficult. Thus they lost the power of relating what they knew to what we knew, and hence, even when fertile in research, were sterile as leaders or guides. Indeed, with one or two notable exceptions, that college faculty as a whole seemed totally unaware that one of the great world changes in social and cultural adjustment was under way in their own country, and that we, as its unripe fruits, were as interesting as any of their specimens and sets of statistics. Not even their historians had observed

that the energies and obsessions and the crude but vital philosophy we reflected even in our play, were part of the great American experiment in competitive individualism which carried so much promise and menace for the modern world. They talked to us as visitors at the Zoo might deal with a jaguar from the jungle, futility and ignorance on either side of the bars. Their neat categories of thinking were cages into which our disorderly and somewhat childish imaginations refused to step. We kept our vigor, our rich loyalty, our faith in a panacea called success. They kept their naive confidence in facts and theory unrelated to the social environment. They talked in a vacuum while we breathed the raw air from outside. They had great power, especially the scientists, who have transformed our mechanisms for living, but this power was exerted upon specialists like themselves. Training technicians successfully, they left human nature to discipline or precept, and let the leaders of society at large educate themselves in college life.

Literature had been my chief interest, even as an undergraduate, and in literature I was then a barbarian and most of my classmates little better than savages. We were favored by having one of the great scholars of our time as teacher. But was he concerned to lift our rawer minds into some perception of beauty, into some idea of the subtlety of life when properly interpreted, or even into a knowledge of values beyond our narrow and youthful experience? I could never discover it. He was a wit, a humanist, a master of sarcasm, a bold and courageous thinker—yet not for us, except when our stupidity aroused his gift for invective. The gulf between our two worlds was too great. He did not wish to cross it; preferred rather to shoot bombards at us from his side of the chasm. And when the enthusiasts beckoned us over, he had shot in his locker for them also.

Discipline and literary history were what we were crammed with, and never a word to indicate that Shakespeare, Dryden, and Goldsmith might have been more interested in us and our glowing faith in progress than in his interpretation of their obscurer passages. I have seen Lounsbury, for it was he, condemn a senior class, unprepared to explain the political allusions of "Absalom and Achitophel," to memorize a chapter of a dull manual of abbreviated literary history. I have witnessed the tireless energy

[94]

with which he lashed the sons of steel and oil and the other owners and managers of America, for a failure to know facts which had as little real reference to literature as to industrialism. It was a good show, mortifying to self-complacency, but destructive of education. He would complain of casting his pearls before swine, yet indeed they were not pearls, though pearls of wisdom he had for others, nor swine, for we were merely full-blooded youths who were from Missouri, needing to be shown the possible relations between what we were and what better men had written out of their richer experience. Lounsbury was a carver's tool used upon unhewn timber. That was not his fault, but the system's, which used his goad, not his brains. He was its instrument in a class warfare, bitter on one side, obstinate on the other. The faculty of that college would not realize that books were made for men, men alive and growing. They studied everything but us. And so we of the student party were like a garrison forced to serve in the academic citadel, but sure to go over later to the enemy. And we did—though carrying some contraband ideas with us.

For there were men on that faculty as capable

as Lounsbury who were resolved that if they could not turn us into scholars at least they would make us think. Such a one was William Graham Sumner, whose pointed ideas landed squarely on that area where American life was already sensitive and was soon to become inflamed. In my time he was the only faculty member that parents feared, the only man that alumni tried to have discharged from his post. Our parents by now were little troubled by evolution and its accompanying materialism, which was to take so many of us away from the churches, for in practice they had anticipated theory by becoming materialists themselves. The even more revolutionary propaganda of science, with its insistence upon expert knowledge, did not disturb them, because they needed experts and were sure that they could control them. But whatever touched their complacent belief that our economic and governmental system could safely be left in the hands of its friends, upset their vials of wrath. Protection (we were most of us Republicans), taxation, capitalism in general, imperialistic war—these sacred bulls should be kept off the college campus, where irreverent theorists might prod them until they broke loose upon the college town and the city beyond it. And with the parents and the alumni most of our faculty secretly or openly agreed. The best education, so they felt, confined itself to nature and let man alone, except in the specimens of his brain work that could be comfortably studied in the records of the past.

With Sumner, nevertheless, was many another, often young and distrusted by the faculty, who sent charges of shot into our unprotected flanks, leaving us sore and somewhat puzzled, since ideas were not what we supposed we were to get from education. But the system was against them. Our college life was for the moment impregnable because it was the romantic essence of current American aspiration. Such men as Sumner could barb it here and there, but the faculty at large who fought us with their own blunt weapons, knowing no more than we what was the real issue, were quite helpless. They comforted themselves by training specialists in compartmented knowledge. As for us, if they had their marking system, we had our college life.

Thus the college faculty lived and worked in a split environment, became accustomed to camouflage, and too easily consented to a compromise in which education was double natured and double faced. This was my first harsh lesson, not too well-learned, when I became myself a teacher and would-be scholar. There was bluff among the students, but bluff in the faculty also; and what was worse, for the older men an intrinsic self-deception from which few escaped. Students and faculty alike learned to salute idealism with one hand while doing what they pleased with the other. The American young animal was singularly healthy then, and his experience had such ample margins that until recently he got along very nicely with a double standard of values. But there is a karma for bluffers. The students met theirs later in the proved insufficiency of their education to meet the tests of a more complicated world. The college professor has encountered his in the disrespect, often undeserved, which has greeted his every emergence from the college seclusion. This was supposed, once, to be due to his relative poverty; but now that poverty is better distributed, one sees it is because his students felt that he was too often a man who professed unrealities. The American college which was not a *collegium* of letters but rather a society for competitive education; nor an association of scholars but rather a coming together of youths preparing to be capitalists; and yet not a utilitarian institution so much as a Utopia for those who later would play all life like a strenuous game: this college, which was not sordid, nor isolated entirely from movements of beauty and the mind, was so impure a mixture that its influences were sure to break up into compounds of unusual intricacy, poisons and explosives among them.

For this one cannot put the blame on the faculty. They were high-minded men. Nor upon college life, which was a true product of the American spirit. Nevertheless it is not surprising if among the results of this college history was an American professor who, like Cassandra, had only to open his mouth in order to be disbelieved. In my day, he prophesied the war, later he prophesied the depression, when it came he described its causes and, with wide divergence in opinion but with a core of unanimous agreement, told what would cure it. He foretells now the need for new bases of morality, the value of standards, the dependence of culture upon literature and art, the urgent necessity of a speedy adaptation of human minds to a new human environment. And few listen because they acquired the habit of not listening in college. He denied their world then; now they cannot believe that he is really concerned with it, or knows what he is talking about. This is one result of a compromise between two educations that were courteous to each other, but never talked the same language, and seldom met in an issue vital to both.

All this was agreeably hidden in a misty future when under rows of elms which still flaunted the optimism of the nineteenth century although the gases of industrialism had poisoned their roots, I gave myself wholeheartedly to *alma mater*, consenting to a dose of formal education with neither complaint nor enthusiasm. But with my first experiences as a novice in the faculty the mists had alarmingly lifted.

CHAPTER V

Teaching

I WAS brought up in a Philistine community where education was one of the lesser public utilities. Teaching as a profession was regarded by my friends and family as a last resort for those who could not do anything else. An obvious explanation, that teaching was poorly paid, did not tell the whole story. The ministry was poorly paid, but met with no such mild but rather deadly disrespect; while dentistry, though profitable, was socially less estimable than teaching.

There seems to have been an idea, not too clearly thought out, that the teacher, even the college teacher, did his work in a childish world from which adult men and women had escaped by taking up the really important tasks of life. The teacher lived on the margin of such vital affairs as business or running a household, and

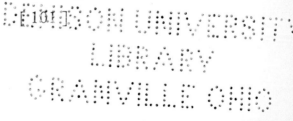

was perhaps not really an adult at all. It was always surprising to learn that a teacher had made money or fallen in love. Teachers were usually high-minded and cultivated people, yet belonged nevertheless among the servile classes, a cut above a nurse. This was what they thought.

And yet the economic explanation was true also. By the beginning of our twentieth century the philosophy of competition had got such a grip upon the American imagination that making money and (with less agreement) spending money, had become a test of success. But a teacher ducked out of the competition at the beginning, which seemed a confession of inferiority. If the teacher was a "she" of course we were more tolerant.

My four years at college did not entirely uproot this vulgar prejudice, although I was shaken by my contacts with a few teachers so powerful that I was forced to regard them as I had been taught to regard other men. Absorbed in college life, which was such a vivid reflection of the competitive economics of the American world outside, we would listen, faintly amused, to dry old men who talked of syntactical irregularities with the high seriousness our fathers reserved for real estate and dividends; and we were often annoyed by the earnestness of lecturers who grew excited over problems that in our home towns were regarded as having no connection with practical life. To the teachers who gained our affection we gave familiar nicknames, such as "Baldy," "Walrus," "Goat," "Speedy"; to those we disliked, less agreeable attributions, such as "Stinker"; but in every case the break-through into recognition of the man behind the professor, seems to have resulted from a surprised discovery that this creature who took astronomy or history so seriously, was after all quite human.

By one of those twists of circumstance which are the tricks chance plays on opinionated man, I found myself, after graduation, confronted with an opportunity to study and teach, the alternatives being business, which I dreaded, or literature, which I felt with reason to be the thinnest of ice for my slender capacities. The influences of the college town, and the unworldly academic life within it, which was so much in accord with my Quaker inheritance, and also the desire for more knowledge which our somewhat casual association with learning had stirred in me, all had made me reluctant to go back to the everyday life which I still regarded as normal. I chose teaching, with no more "call" to it than had my cousins at home to the bankers' and manufacturers' offices they entered as a matter of course. And so, uncorrupted by theories, untouched by the missionary spirit, unimpressed as yet by the nobility of an intellectual career, like a colt straying toward a new pasture where the grass looked green and the gate was open, I slipped into one of the six great professions.

This is no autobiography. I use personal experience only because it is my evidence for the value of the college experience that formed our generation. I am more concerned with truth in interpretation than with fidelity to the actual happening. Nevertheless, I think that my own history as a member of such a faculty as I have described in the last chapter, is significant because my ascent as a teacher from careless ignorance to eager interest and finally to spiritual agitation, gave me the wobbling course of one slow to know his own mind, and made me more sensitive to the issues involved than my more fortunate colleagues who, like the boy on the burning deck, knew precisely what they had to do, and did it. I was the first in nine known generations of a family to enter a profession, I was the first from my circle of friends and relatives to escape from the profits system. I came into the faculty from the college with a traditional respect for the bourgeois American's creed of business as the chief concern of normal man, and with something reaching out from my mind toward ideals of scholarship, and something shrinking back by habit from the practitioners thereof, whose language, manners, humor or lack of it, and ideas of success in life, I was not yet prepared to understand. Gulliver felt somewhat as I did, when landing upon Laputa he found that factories made learning, and conversation was about mathematics instead of money and love.

Very early in my career, which in its beginning was humble in the extreme—and fortunately so since I knew just enough to keep one jump ahead of my classes—I brought my father to the club in our college town. He was to meet two of my superiors, elder statesmen in education for whom I had a profound respect. My father was the sweetest and most equable of men, deeply cultured in simple human relationships, but not accustomed to discussions where ideas were passed about wantonly and encyclopedic facts

[105]

spilled as if everyone had plenty of them. The elder statesmen were bored, and my father was puzzled although he did his best to find something in his very American experience which would provide a meeting-place. As he flushed, looking more and more to me for help, a tiny idea was born in my mind of the true nature of this profession of teaching. It was a resultant of the inevitable conflict between theory and practice; it was built upon the ultimate duty of scholarship to give what was needed, and made doubly difficult by the inability or the refusal of human nature to take what it lacked and the failure of the teacher to measure his task. That day I saw for the first time the teacher's real problem—and for twenty years blundered on, ill-prepared and often mistaken, and sometimes successful, and more often self-deluded, yet, like all real teachers, hopeful, on its trail.

For I think that teaching as a profession is woefully misunderstood, and frequently by its professors. Perhaps I should qualify this statement to read teaching of the humanities, which I know most about, yet I do not feel inclined to qualify it. It may be that teaching a technique such as playwriting or the building of bridges is a simple matter hard to misunderstand, yet I am quite sure that the instant the subject taught is used for training and expanding the mind the problem is much more complex than the simple formula: I know this, I tell it to you, now you know it—which seems to be what most laymen regard as teaching.

I never taught playwriting or metal work, but I have raised my temperature and strained my wits in the teaching of both English literature and English composition, with brief excursions into history and even logic. What I am surest of is, that what I tried to teach was never so important as how I taught it. I can conceive of no subject of instruction so important that a pupil cannot get along without it, except reading, writing, and arithmetic, unless it be ethics and religion, which few teach nowadays. Of course the race has to have the sciences if it is to keep up its standard of living, architects must have calculus, and classicists Latin, but I am writing of the individual. What *he* needs is not necessarily Greek, or physics, or geography, but an education.

My first discovery when, as a sallow-faced instructor in a black felt hat and very Puritan clothing (the fashion for academic intellectuals in the early 1900s), I began my career, was that education is more concerned with ideals than with knowledge, a naive discovery, but important. I never had the usual difficulties of young instructors, though I dreamed of them in tutor's nightmares, in which ink flew through the air while I escaped in my shirt tails through a window. I was slight physically, unaccustomed to authority, unsure of my subject, uncertain in my methods. Nevertheless no class "rough-housed" me (a word of the period); when dogs were brought into my recitation they promptly went to sleep; when fisticuffs started on the back row I had only to throw a question in that direction. Yet I nerved myself for my classes as for an ordeal, and relapsed after them into limp vacuity. For I quickly learned, intuitively, crudely, yet I learned, that whether it was the history of the English language, or Shakespeare, that I was trying to teach, the actual conflict was not with ignorance but with college life and all that it implied; and behind it the ideas and ideals of an American society in which materialism dominated action and governed thought. One could plant facts by waving a mark book, but when it came to ideas, beliefs, ideals, the soil was stubborn.

There were five schools of the theory of teaching in my day: the hard-boiled, the indifferent, the idealistic, the factual, and the enthusiastic.

The hard-boiled school I respected, yet something in their tenets made me stubbornly rebellious. There was a Cambridge graduate on our faculty, an Englishman older than myself, with whom I argued over many a stein of beer. We have the stuff, he would say, let the little lambs come and get it if they wish. If they are goats who won't eat good food, that is their affair. I can give them good mathematics, and if they want mathematics I will work with them. If they don't, why should I coddle them!

And so he saved his emotions for high struggles with figured thinking, bred a few good students, made a reputation for his scholarship, and got through his teaching with only the labor required to talk clearly for fifty minutes.

I tried to feel his way. I knew that we coddled the undergraduate. I was aware that we tried to wheedle our doses of instructions, like cod liver oil, into his unwilling mouth between his hearty feedings on college life. I felt that if

I could stand on a pedestal, like my Cambridge friend, saying "I have it, come and get it, or stay away," I should be more respected and so would my subject. But I believed that those I most wanted to teach would never come because they would never understand why they should come. My American tradition held me back from such downrightness. After all, our job had been, and was, to educate all of the people. If it was not incumbent upon me to teach Anglo-Saxon to guttersnipes, yet what right had I to keep Shakespeare and Milton for the tiny minority of American undergraduates who would take to them naturally, who would read them with a self-determined resolve to understand? The specialist might be hard-boiled, and properly so. The Englishman might be exclusive, for in England education had always been regarded as a privilege, and hence a specialty. With us, education was what religion had been to our ancestors, something to be spread abroad to all who had minds that could be saved. Which meant that those who felt as I did worked harder over a weary football player, or a perfectly cynical broker's son, than with the fine minds already lit with enthusiasm for learning which we were sure to find somewhere in our classes. With the natural result that our energies were exhausted in trying to educate the almost uneducatable, while in any faculty meeting the discussion never got far from the lame ducks and the bluffers, and what to do about low marks.

The indifferent school of teachers had long since accepted the hopelessness of this endless siege of undergraduate interest. Without admitting it, least of all to themselves, they had become defeatists in education. The academic life was pleasant—long summers, short hours, easy requirements for the unambitious once they were placed, abundant opportunities for spending sensibly and agreeably a private income if you were fortunate enough to have one. Nor did a man have to teach or to write with distinction in order to get his job and hold it in that society which was so agreeable to the cultivated mind. There were innumerable committees needing executive talent, there were sports to be supervised, rules to be made, morale to be seen to. And there was the curriculum, which, like the power plant of a factory, had to be overhauled or redesigned every other year. A personable man of character could keep himself reasonably busy through an academic lifetime without doing one hour of really effective teaching, or writing one page that lifted beyond routine. He became, so to speak, a dean or president without portfolio and without real educational responsibility, and was often better known, and more quickly rewarded, than the true scholar or the born teacher, whose light shone less abroad among the alumni and in the college town.

Nor was the siege of the undergraduate mind necessarily unpleasant once the besieging became an end in itself. These indifferents imitated medieval warfare. Against a wall of resistance they threw up another wall of requirements, behind which they lived very comfortably while the conflict remained in *status quo*. Boredom encountered routine, dullness met dullness, irresponsibility was checked by the marking system, and a technique was developed guaranteed to produce the expected number of grades which would test at passing or just above. Many a good man went down this sterile road in college teaching, was useful, respected, and did a little bit of everything about the college shop except educate or contribute to thinking. There they had accepted defeat. And if many college generations were bored to extinction in their classes, the wheels of college routine ran smoother thanks to such men. And if scholarship went forward never a millimetre by their efforts, at least they made no minor errors, pursued no lost causes, did no damage to convention, and proved to the suspicious American world outside that a professor could be as much of a good fellow, and as harmless, as a vice-president of a bank. Yet I fear they were not harmless. Their dead hand rests on many a mind yet.

As for the idealists, I wonder if I have the right name for them. Such a bull-headed generation I have never known in any other profession, for daily they went out to fight for their ideas, and daily they were defeated. And yet stupid as some of them were, and blind as to what was going on and the source of their difficulties, as were most, I cannot but feel that they were the only realists in the college of my day. Obstinately determined to make what they thought was truth prevail, they alone intuitively saw, or at least felt and dimly perceived, college education for what it essentially was—a battle with the natural cussedness, consistent short-sightedness, and obstinate resistance of the human animal to whatever uncomfortably raises him above the brute. They were much too dogmatic, much too inexperienced in life, very much too cerebral in their theories and naive in their emotions, to be often entirely right. But they were on the right side of education even when they were absurdly wrong in their estimates of what their young animals needed. They were on the only side that really wanted a victory.

I numbered my best friends among the idealists, yet it was extraordinary how widely we differed in items of belief. Some of them, having hitched their wagons to an earlier century, were concerned only with the fallacies of our own. They had certain advantages over the rest of us who felt that the nineteen hundreds were of considerable importance since it was clear that we should have to do our living in them. A complete faith in the *mores* of, let us say, the age of Dr. Johnson, produced eventually in the teacher who felt that way, a character so eccentric from our *mores* as to fascinate modern youth by his very difference. His arguments also had the force of resting upon a precedent of glamorous living. Instead of feeble remonstrances against the trivial and the sensational in our college life, where football practice or trying to make a fraternity engaged our best energies, these praisers of old days could throw wits, beauties, and statesmen at the student head, and show life fully lived in a manner so different as to challenge the dullest intelligence.

Other idealists of my acquaintance were soaked in romantic moralism. Literature was written, according to them, to illustrate the vices and virtues. Shakespeare proved that character made fate, and the lyrics of Tennyson were less "significant" than his sermons in verse. Their students were not surprised; they had been taught that way in school, yet felt that they had been betrayed when spot passages from ribald scenes in Shakespeare or lyric lines that obviously contained no moral philosophy, were put upon the examination papers. How the devil were you to interpret morally a jest of Falstaff, or the verses

> *Courtesied when you have and kissed*
> *The wild waves whist.*

I was cured myself of using all English literature as an exercise in Victorian morality by reading aloud to my class a line of Tennyson's that permitted, and did not fail to get, and with hysterical laughter, a bawdy interpretation. The relief was so obvious that I knew instantly I had been preaching not teaching. I realized with a saving humor that good literature was far too human to make sermons of, though sermons it might often contain, far too human to be made into a diet of oughts and ought nots. And I soon concluded that we who squeezed ethics from our teaching of literature or history, were dodging the far more difficult task of making the culture of the past at home in the imagination of the undergraduate.

The factual teachers were the happiest. They were competent men who knew every detail of their subjects. For them teaching was a job in agriculture. Break up the field of the mind by threats of ploughing its wild oats under. Plant the seeds of honest fact—declensions, dates, formulas. Reap the crop at examination time, and woe to the boy with an empty basket. The system would have been perfect, if it had not been for the complete lack of fertilizer. The grain came back to the farmer not hundred fold, but one in a hundred, and that one often mouldy.

Nevertheless, the factual was the school of

teaching most popular among the faculty; naturally so, for it could do no harm, and since facts in all subjects were the indispensable beginnings of wisdom, might do more good than the uncertainties of theorizing and interpretation. Facts could stimulate also, and there was little danger that they would stimulate too much.

But my God!—what masses of facts I have heard poured out in the classroom! How many facts, more or less accurate, I myself have dumped on my classes! What myriads of alleged facts I have read in test papers! There is something sane and sensible about a fact. Given the coefficients, can you or can you not plot a curve? Do you or do you not know the relative dates of Charlemagne and El Mansur? Why did the crustaceans fail to evolute like man? What happened when Horatio met Hamlet after the latter's escape from the pirates? If I were to go back to general teaching again I should either break my forehead anew on the old stone wall erected ages since to shut out ideas and ideals, or happily and wholeheartedly go in for facts. The teaching of linguists must be joyful for it is nearly all facts. An hour with a good list of factual questions to propose is like a game—ends too like a game with the score 0-0 but a grand sensation of having played hard. I have seen one of my own professors become so fascinated with the sport of dropping queries like depth bombs here and there, that he forgot to mark, forgot to dismiss, his sweating class. There is an immense satisfaction in the concrete for both teacher and taught. The well-crammed youngster is like a siphon bottle. Press the handle and he fizzes in a welcome relief from pressure. And the happy professor well supplied with hard questions of fact is like the gardener who whiffs spray on a plant and sees the worm turn up his belly in a just agony.

It was facts I began to teach, and never afterwards did I have more efficient recitations. There was a sporting atmosphere in the classroom life of the early nineteen hundreds. Of the "prof" it was expected that he would prepare shrewd questions touching upon hidden deposits of fact easily missed in preparation unless by chance the student had an old book with arrows inked in pointing to the treasure. The teacher asked: the pupil replied. He said he did not know, which was zero. He gave the right answer, which in our mystic marking system counted four. Or he entered upon a rambling disquisition which was meant, and intended to be understood, as a bluff. Could teacher corner him into making a statement of fact, which was sure to be wrong? If he could, that also was zero. If teacher could not catch him out, the sporting code required that he should get a complimentary two, which was passing, and he complained if he did not receive it. The class, expert in games, if not in the subject of instruction, watched the struggle, excited sometimes to the point of groans or applause.

I was cured of the factual method as a major sport in education, by a slender, sensitive youngster who had been educated by private tutors abroad. He was too intent upon his own thinking to answer directly my simple question as to what Prince Hal thought of Falstaff, by which of course I meant what he *said* he thought. Instead, as one interested mind to another, he began what was, by definition, clearly a bluff, yet soon became a query as to whether Shakespeare himself was not, like all playwrights, prone to bluff, letting speeches stand from history which he had been too lazy to rewrite. The class, which had set him down for a two, withdrew their favor when he went on with the discussion for the sake of an argument, which he seemed to take more seriously than his mark. But I, with my neat questions to test laborious reading all pat, felt like a fool, and was one. The happy solace of asking contentedly, "Was it?" and hearing "It was" or "It wasn't," the day's duty thus done, was never more mine. And yet I did not forget, nor do I forget here, that it is upon fact that tradition by which alone we safely live, rides from the past into the present.

I have already mentioned the enthusiastic school of teaching, but welcome the chance to speak of it again in a different setting. It was a school to which I would gladly have been inspired. The enthusiast was a peculiar product of the *fin de siècle*. One encountered him usually in the humanities, but there were scientists and even teachers of language who belonged in this category, and in my day so cold and hard a subject as physics was then, boasted of one. I have said that in the more skeptical present the enthusiast has been ranked with the revivalists. Actually he was a by-product of revivalism, which the great days of Moody and Sankey and William Booth had made infectious to educated men. But the educated men in our day were not often attracted to religion. Religion was either too dogmatic for them or too emotional. Herbert Spencer had destroyed the prestige of theology, and they were well aware that William James had described conversion as a phenomenon of psychology. Hence many with a fire of enthusiasm for the good, the beautiful, and the true turned to art, to the wonders of nature, and most of all to literature. One could be enthusiastic about Shakespeare when it had already become a little vulgar to be enthusiastic about being saved. Even the technique was the same, and familiar comparisons, good stories, histrionics, were as effective in lectures upon Shelly as in rantings upon the Blood of the Lamb.

The students responded. In these men so fired with the excitements of their subject, so keen to show others that poetry or evolution or philology was life abstrated but intensified, they recognized a rebellion against the formalism they also hated, and a sympathetic relationship with their own easy enthusiasms in college life. And yet I could never become one of the enthusiasts, though I owed much to them. What this kind of teaching required was a special gift which was not so much oratory or histrionics as an uncritical faith in the miracle of knowledge.

When they spoke of what they loved, life for their hearers seemed more vivid, more conscious than before. That was good, but it did not come by mere telling. There had to be transferred emotion, and the emotion, unless it was simple, could not be easily transferred, not even by a revivalist. It required a special secretion of simple, intense minds, with a genius for communication. The enthusiasts were born not made. They were our prima donnas, who triumphed even when their voices went sharp or flat of the truth.

And when they had done their work the soil was ploughed up but not planted. They made learning seem desirable, but left it an emotion and a mystery. They gave their hearts, but few ideas with them. Their converts did not relapse, like the drunkards and prostitutes won by the revivalists; they remained friends to culture, but stopped there unless someone took them further along the road. And yet in that boisterous college, with its tacit agreement that only mirth and social success really counted, to be a friend of culture was an achievement. As a young teacher I could never let myself go in the kind of enthusiasm that sent classes home burning to read

everything from the Koran to "Dorian Gray,"
because I was uncomfortably aware of how little
I knew of the realities that explained both Mo-
hammed and Oscar Wilde. Yet I envied those
who had no inhibitions in their passion for
books—any books. I felt for them the gratitude
and reluctant admiration of Hamlet for the actor
who wept over Hecuba. That fellow got his
audience, and so did they.

I cast my lot, therefore, with the idealists,
which name I now discard, as being inaccurate,
and call them the philosophic in teaching, a sect
which has always persisted in the crooked but
fascinating road of education, although many
of its followers in the past have, like my humble
self, had little claim to be called philosophers.
Yet what is philosophy in practice but wondering what it is all about, with a passion for trying
to discover?

The college teacher, especially if he is young,
has a curious human experience, both intimate
and remote. He sits half the day examining
minds at just the age when they have reached full
intelligence and yet cannot either entirely conceal
or entirely reveal their texture. He has boys and
girls of the best age for playing upon, and they

are a picked youth, if not always picked for his especial purposes. And they are charming, more than ever before, more than ever afterwards. Outside the classroom they become easily his friends, though never really intimate; inside they are deferential, even in their determination to resist knowledge, and often frank in what they say, though their inner lives are infinitely withdrawn. They bring their background with them, and not their words so much as their wills are intensely expressive. Teaching such a class is like lifting a thin and waving plank. It is never steady, always ready to bend and fall;—an instant's release of the grip and it is down to earth.

In my day we sat on a raised dais with thirty or more youngsters sprawled beneath us. It was like an established church where the pastor, hired to save souls, faces a congregation that has come because it is Sunday. We seated the students alphabetically, making for our own use a pencilled plan of the seats, each of which was numbered, and writing on it the names of the students in their assigned locations. Thus when "Townsend" was called, the six feet of shambling drowsiness needing a pinch which rose to its feet, could be readily identified. Without this simple device there was always the chance that some little Russian Jew would grab an easy question and sell his knowledge for an A.

At first one's class was a sea of faces, pimply, vacuous, keen, sulky, and amiable, all dissolving into a blur of washed and rosy youth. But soon (and Buddhist priests and doctors of the Sorbonne must have had the same experience), the room disintegrated into familiar types. The pleasantest, I think, was the well mannered, neatly dressed boy from the orthodox preparatory schools. He was deferential to teacher, polite to the scrawny high-school boy beside him. Yet he was still all boy and at each moment of relaxation would tickle his schoolmate on the other side, and be slyly punched in return, the two of them like puppies trying hard not to roll over and cuff and bite. Yet put those well trained boys on the football field where serious life for them began, and they would tackle low, and slug and viciously kick when the umpire was not looking. A faint aroma of cereal and cream exuded from these preparatory school boys. They had nice mothers and generous fathers. Their world was already made for them, and, like blooded colts, they were expected to play, because their future work was to be a fierce competition to make the family richer. They had the arrogance and the gentleness of the aristocrat, without his detachment from life. They were being groomed for the capture or retention of privilege, and its enjoyment. Every one of them expected to start in business or professional life at the bottom and to come to the top as easily as he rushed a ball past untrained opponents. The type was Spartan rather than Athenian; and, like the Spartans, they were quite inaccessible to new ideas, having closed their minds at sixteen or seventeen upon a code of success which left no room for speculation.

These fine boys with their good voices, their courtesy and self-assurance, would sit out the hour in deferential boredom, then, at the word of dismissal, crowd the doorway in a sudden release of energy, leaving the young teacher in an agony of frustration. For they had everything—health, good looks, will, character, reserves of energy—everything but open minds, everything but cracks in their stiff brains into which ideas could flow! With consummate skill gained in long experience with clever teachers and the right text books, they gave to Caesar exactly what Caesar was supposed to get from them, the modicum of facts, the statements of the last lecture reduced to a formula, enough to get a B in Freshman year when the footing was still unsteady, just enough for a C in Senior year when the danger of flunking was past. You liked them as you like blooded show dogs. Like show dogs they defeated every attempt to teach their well-bred intellect new tricks.

Scattered here and there in every class were the "grinds," called by the preparatory school dilettantes either "greasy grinds" or just "grinds." Actually the differences between the two varieties were subtle. The typical grind was a survival of the old college that trained chiefly for teaching and the ministry. He was usually the quiet and bloodless member of a family, afraid of rough sports, averse to competition, seeking refuge in books. His face was blank, his mind was a sponge which squeezed dry and filled again without cellular change. The young teacher found him trying, since he did everything he was told, believed all he heard, studied everything assigned to him, and at the end wrote papers that were correct with a deathly perfection of the commonplace which showed how ineffective education could be unless it touched the emotions, of which he had none.

The "greasy grind" was a racial or social variant of the plain grind. The greasy grind seldom changed his collar. He had a sneaking cleverness which taught him to snap up the hard questions in easy courses, thus collecting high marks as a protection against a world that, quite properly, wished to keep him down. He would argue with teacher for ten minutes trying to get a B changed into an A; but he had no intellectual curiosity. Education for him was a coin, useless unless you could buy something with it. The dilettante could sometimes be shocked into a realization that there were other worlds than his, and so other values in living; but the greasy grind was both unchangeable and inescapable, a fly buzzing about your weary head.

Another and very different type of industrious student in those classes is well recognized now, but was then regarded by the pink and well soaped elect as just another undesirable. The second generation from the East of Europe was beginning to come to college:—Polish Jews with anemic faces on which were set dirty spectacles, soft-eyed Italians too alien to mix with an

Anglo-Saxon community, seam-faced Armenian
boys, and now and then a Chinese.   These, except the last, were all in college to learn how to
live in America.   Their mien was apologetic; you
could see them watching with envious curiosity
the courteous indifference of the superior race;
they took little part in discussions, and asked
for no credit.   Yet often their more flexible
minds could be felt playing round and round
the confident Anglo-Saxons, admiring, skeptical,
puzzled, and sometimes contemptuous.   Occa-
sionally there would be a revelation of intellect
or a hint of the future, when some Chinese boy,
caught off his guard, and forgetting the convention of the classroom which was to answer a
question and sit down, would give a précis of
the entire lesson, and perhaps the previous one
and the next, which only a French intellectual
could have equalled.   Or some Russian Jewish
exile, asked to comment on an Ibsen play, and
losing control of his guarded intellect, would
expound a social philosophy that made the class
squirm as if a blast of fire had scorched the seats
of their comfortable pants.

Every class had also its freaks, which in those
college days was a familiar term with a definite

meaning. And nothing could have better revealed the nature of our college community than the diversity of types which were all called, for convenience, and to indicate their difference from the true-blue college men, freaks. A freak was a nonconformist. He might be a preparatory school boy of good family who had failed somehow to take the right impress from the preparatory school mould. He might be, and often was, a son of the very rich, or of artistic bohemians, who had been educated in Europe, and was ill at ease in our Philistine Zion. He might be a potential homosexual distracted by his own unrecognized perversity. He might be, but rarely was, a little crazy. Sometimes he was merely an adult intellect in the society of adolescents, who refused to waste his time in organized athletics, although obviously competent, who declined fraternity elections, and was obsessed by a morbid interest in chemistry or philology. All such were freaks.

The Spartan parallel again holds good, since the arts in this question of freakishness were especially suspect. To be musical and indulge in music privately was a sure sign of freakishness, as bad as private drinking or the reading of poetry in seclusion. The banjo, the mandolin, and the guitar were respectable, since skilful players could "make" the instrumental clubs and so gain social recognition; but proficiency on the violin was a sure sign of something wrong, as was skill on the piano not confined to "beating the box," and also the singing of "classic" music. Radical ideas, a taste for the society of professors, silk pyjamas, an interest in art, careful English, long hair (except on football heroes), uncollegiate clothes, and a lack of interest in sports, all designated the freak, who was a person dangerous to make friends with. Only religion, thanks to our evangelical heritage, was allowed eccentricities of self-expression, for it was a part of the code.

Hence the young teacher, himself a mild nonconformist since otherwise he would never have gone into teaching, was often embarrassed by the sudden drop in classroom temperature when, misled or ignorant, he gave a freak the floor and his approval. The boy who looked at him with dumb, devoted eyes, the boy who compared Milton to Bach, the youth who knew the Italian primitives in the Art School, the freak who asked whether Christ was not a good socialist, and the exquisite who actually articulated his English, and quoted French in a foreign accent—call upon anyone of these and all motion forward was stopped for that day. An Alexandrian Greek could have met with no more disapproval if asked to address the Conscript Fathers of the Roman republic.

I soon grew accustomed to this so variegated class, learning to play one faction against another, soap, so to speak, against dirty finger nails, agile intellect against the solidity of a confident code. Yet what saved those of us who tried to be philosophers in our role of teaching, was another, and fortunately unfailing, contribution from America to our college classes. I remember well those first days of each teaching year: the confident moment when one looked down upon fresh faces in the old seats, and hoped that this time at last faith would be justified. And then the quick disillusion as the herd rounded up into the same old assortment of mavericks, mixed breeds, and stolid beef cattle. Yet as with ranging question and hopeful reading of test papers we sifted and searched, always in some unexpected corners would be found those quiet minds, tenacious, reserved, cautious, practical, and yet ready to sight an idea and pursue it, and apply it,

and keep faith with it—not speculative. not logical, but unshakeable in confidence that most problems can be solved—which are the best products of the great American experiment. Sometimes it was character, sometimes it was sanity, sometimes it was intellectual courage which is very different from intellectual daring, that one found and relied upon to give some coherence to the struggle to civilize such discordant elements when oneself was so imperfectly civilized.

I never failed to get such minds in my classes but once. Then I was assigned to a division of "repeaters," boys who were being allowed to go through their deficient Freshman work again in order that their invaluable services on various teams or managerships, or as merry drunkards, should be retained at least until Christmas. And then the issue was so clear, David against Goliath, with only a sling when he needed a machine gun, that the class became a match conducted in high good humor, and with rules observed by both sides, according to which it was agreed that if I caught them they were out; with the result that a side wave from the strenuous competitions of college life washed through that classroom, football leviathans memorized Shakespeare and liked him, and boozers defended Falstaff. A committee waited on me at the end of the year, saying that I had been a good sport, and offering to teach me an infallible method for catching bluffers before they got to home plate.

I met one of that class last year, a good-natured broker, fat now and a little seedy since 1929. "I remember your class," he said. "It's the only one I do remember. I got to like that guy Hamlet. I meant to read more about him some time. But you know how it is—I had to work when I quit college."

They all intended to work, when they left college. That was why teaching in those days was exciting. There was no belief in the student's mind that what you taught had any vital relation with real work, or, for that matter, with real life. You felt, and rightly, that it might be the last chance to bring them into contact with any values not purely utilitarian.

I wondered then, but do not wonder now, at that excitement, which kept us, the young teachers, talking, brooding, dreaming over our job, which after all was miserably paid, little respected, and three quarters of it a routine as dull as a clerk's. With the added psychological danger of acquiring arrogance, pedantry, and dogmatism, which are the occupational diseases of those who spend their lives directing the intellects of the young.

I do not wonder now, because it is so clear that we were on the firing line. The pre-Civil War culture of the East had grown stale or genteel. The colleges were filled with the second generation of the industrial pioneers, who had been brought up in a tradition of laissez-faire and the devil catch the hindmost. The boys we faced were nourished on a great illusion, and so well nourished that there was room for little else in their minds. They believed with that implicit faith which is so much more powerful than doctrine, that the rest of their lives would be spent in a Great Struggle for wealth and privilege, where the best grabbers would win, and where only freaks and dreamers would take time to speculate upon what it was all about and whether the result was happiness. The heir to a banker's million was just as much under the spell of the necessity to be strenuous as the son of a Jewish pants-presser. Indeed if anything, it was the well born and wealthy who were surest that making money was essential for their safety and would mean for them success.

And since the country was really behind them, and the times favored their ambitions, while the churches had lost their hold upon idealism, or, like the Y. M. C. A., praised such success as the only antidote to the vices of idleness, we young teachers were forced to play the part of Isaiahs preaching another God than Mammon. Irritated by our helplessness, we would make sermons out of poetry and tracts for the times from prose that was meant to be delightful. Or puzzled and discouraged, we would yield to the current tendency, and turn our classrooms into doctor's offices where bad children were given stiff doses that were sure to do them good. Or we would get through with the whole routine as easily as possible so that we could attend to our own affairs which often were quite as materialistic as the steel business or corporation law.

But sometimes some of us went at it differently, and disillusioned, skeptical, defeated, fought for our ideals again and again with an intensity that was almost lyrical. We knew that the struggle was between two views of civilization, between two ideas of living, between two types of mind, variants of the tender and the tough. It was our feeble repetition of an age-long conflict—Plato versus John Rockefeller, Shakespeare versus Benjamin Franklin, Milton against the stock exchange and the Y. M. C. A. This we felt, and that was why an instructor in English on $1500 a year was often a happy man.

CHAPTER VI

The Academic Life

THE academic life in which these teachers moved and had their being has never, I believe, been psychologically considered, except in a few novels. I do not wish to write of it here in any psycho-analytic fashion for I am far more interested in its values than in its quips, its quiddities, its lesions, and its releases. Yet, regarded as a habit of life and a state of mind, the campus communities were unquestionably an additional state in the bustling America of the early nineteen hundreds. They were a society within the commonwealth, like the Quakers of the eighteenth century, and they lived in oases of relative peace while the rest of the country was madly building roads for progress whose ultimate destination had never been mapped.

Thoughtful spirits who in that confident and aggressive age paused for reflection, were aware of a tension which was more complex than Theodore Roosevelt's cult of strenuosity. It was a tension between ideals, which had reached our college classrooms, and was the cause of that struggle between teacher and taught described in earlier chapters. There was an antagonism between those who wished to know and those eager to do, that grew stronger and more confused as the great industrial age of America mounted toward its peak. It was a conflict between gods and giants, very academic gods it seems to me now, who would have liked to turn the United States into a vast university, and very well-meaning giants who, like Carnegie, said they got rich only to benefit mankind. And

. . . friend and foe were shadows in the mist,
And friend slew friend not knowing whom he
*   slew.*

Yet a battle is a bad simile. As I look back to that cock-sure society of the turn of the century it seems that thinkers and doers, big and little, were, on the whole, very well satisfied with their country and themselves. The tension was there, but everyone supposed it would disappear just as soon as we had made a perfect state—which, whatever else it was going to become, would be prosperous with bigger and better factories and bigger and better dormitories. So the gods and the godlings kept on educating the children, or trying to, according to their lights, and the giants and their office force kept on paying the bills and offering our graduates jobs which required a very different set of ideals from ours. Meanwhile most of us, inside and out of the college, took this dual world for granted. Now and then there was a hint that some day this gentleman's agreement would be broken. I remember the vague uneasiness of my father when the first Roosevelt slid into the presidency. He was a college graduate. His ideas might be bad for business. And behind the vehement anti-imperialism of the Spanish War years and the Philippine settlement, was the instinct that profit was becoming our master. I suppose that the analogy which best describes the relation of academic life to the country at large is the medieval state, in which the monasteries, supported by the community and enriched by predatory king or baron, provided harborage for men violently opposed to the world that permitted them to exist. By that tension Chris-

tianity was shaped and from it came some of our
greatest literature. Our tension was less obvious
and less violent, but it also had results not easily
estimated.

Academic life in America was, and is, pecul-
iarly different from the habits of the rest of the
community. The professor has only a few set
hours and often works at home, much to the
annoyance of his wife. Most of his tasks are self-
set, half of his labor is with milky youth and the
other half with books whose authors are usually
long since dead. He heads away from competition, and his most tense moments may come in
the silence of his study. He may walk when he
pleases under the quiet of the elms; yet he must
never forget that he is a professor, giving example
to youth.

These are his circumstances. The spiritual
difference is much greater and is best understood
by pursuing the comparison with the medieval
state. Our college was an adaptation of the
monastic system, a refuge for the contemplative
and the analytical in a community devoted to the
pursuit of prosperity. But it was the monasticism of an industrial democracy, where the modern monks had to take the democratic burden of

general education, so that the scholar who retired from the world must meet its offspring every morning in the classroom.

No wonder then that the academic community became a true society, different at heart as well as in manners from the rest of the country, and attracting minds that were different from their neighbors', and making different men of them. Not all of these were seekers, eager to advance the intellect. Many were mere escapists from the strenuous life of industrial competition. Some were mild sadists who took their pleasure in tormenting helpless youth. Others were seeking in education the opportunities they no longer found in the weakening churches. And some were drawn into the academic field by a sense for the decencies of living which could be had in a community where there was leisure for those shrewd or rich enough to take it, and wide intellectual and esthetic experience for minds capable of a culture both broad and deep. For all such the academic community was a life as well as a career, and that is why its conditionings toward strength and weakness have been so considerable that one wonders why the historians (who themselves are academic products) have been so little concerned with this state within a state, in which some hundreds of thousands of better-class Americans have in our time acquired qualities as recognizable as a priest's cassock or a soldier's uniform.

As I think over the college town of that pre-war age which I knew best, it seems to have offered to many types of mind the best life, potentially, that America then possessed. Those quiet streets still reminiscent of the early nineteenth century, the vaulted college library redolent of old leather bindings and peaceful as an island, days whose rhythm was steady yet so much more varied than the routine of an office, since the excitement of teaching succeeded quiet study and was followed by tennis or eager walking up Tutor's Lane in high-spirited talk; then nights by the lamp or in a circle earnestly arguing. And those long, long summers in the heart of the country, the active business of education folded away at Commencement, and time all one's own, not to idle, for the prick of ambition was always sharp, but free hour upon hour to sink into books, to wrestle with ideas, to collate, analyze, ponder, and to write. There was no life like it for a man who wished to think and know.   It seemed the antithesis but was really a parallel, to the life of hard work spiced by adventure which was just reaching its end on the frontier of the West.

There was also, even for the young and unplaced, an extraordinary independence in this academic life, limited in its scope, but deeply genuine—and particularly for the young men who still were content with simple living.   I will not say that our minds were free, for our academic conventions bound them, yet of these we were unaware, and within their limits we were not only free, we were urged, to independent thinking.   And our daily life, even in term time, was independent, a source of great content. What a young teacher could do or could not do was also strictly regulated by convention.   Yet in the all important area of authority and the control of time we had privileges which only those who have lost them can truly estimate.   My teaching hours were fixed, but they were few in the day; and if what I taught was in general terms prescribed, how I taught it was my own responsibility.   Each lecture, each recitation, was, if I wished and was able to make it so, a creative task, my own, and undictated.   What relations I chose to have with my students, what disciplines, what intimacies, were of my own devising. I was only a cog in a machine, but my cog was free-wheeling, which was one reason why the college ran with such eccentricity.

And outside of my teaching hours and an occasional committee or faculty meeting, my time was my own to organize. Self-dependence was not only a privilege, it was a requisite. My mind, which theoretically belonged in its intellectual fruitfulness, if any, to the university, was left to my own initiative and my own discipline, to enfeeble or to develop. This was no clerk's or laborer's life. I was, in a very real sense, a man at the helm of his own voyage.

All this led to a pleasant eccentricity of living. There were professors who, like owls, were seen outside their classrooms only at night, keeping lonely vigil with their thoughts, while their reluctant muscles pumped out a mile of disciplinary exercise. There were men whose modishness expressed itself in an Oxford falsetto or the fashions of the undergraduate tailors. And others were like my own chief, now a distinguished figure in public life, who in those early days kept every angle of his Connecticut accent, and never wore a coat, waistcoat, and trousers which matched.

Most of this academic community had led protected lives, and many of them were ignorant of the most vital concerns of the present. In their morals, there was as much meanness, backbiting, subterfuge, and cowardice as in the outside world,—as much, no more. There was much more jealousy, a feminine jealousy, not outspoken, but consuming, hid under masks of dignity, and speaking, when it did speak, always in high terms of ideals to be served and standards to be upheld. I have heard of a professor so insanely jealous of his colleagues that he wrote down his true opinions of them in his will; and I believe the story for I knew a scientist once whose face would flush at the mention of a popular English professor, and whose forehead veins would swell dangerously at the mere word philosophy—philosophy that led his students away skating over thin ice which would not hold his literal intellect.

More significant was their mental range and elevation. These men who had chosen to live and quarrel together in the academic life were by necessity concerned with thinking, and thinking in many categories. For them each chance encounter on the street was a contact with a different kind of knowledge. Not even the laziest minds were bound by the usual male limitations of the day to money making, because there was no profit for them except that which came from their job of study and teaching of subjects which usually had nothing to do with money. Even the laziest minds among them were perforce in contact daily with better minds than theirs—in books. If the tone of our academic society, even when in relaxation at the club, was a little arid, it was the aridity of a high sweeping plateau. And since abstractions are the object of all study, no matter how petty might be our own egoes the dullest and most pedantic among us had to busy himself constantly with the concerns of the human race. We talked details of academic shop until our wives went to bed in boredom, for shop-talk was the irresistible vice that got us all; yet at least when this talk rose above gossip the subject was the getting and acquiring of knowledge, which is certainly a more interesting theme than life insurance or manufacturing. You can be just as dull over education as over advertising or sausage making, but the first has the broader implications.

This academic life was not really arid unless an arid mind made it so. It was enriched and kept moist by that curious absorption between opposites which makes a nation victorious in war take over the attributes of its enemy. We shared the light-heartedness, the loyalty, and the sociability of our nearest approach to an enemy, the undergraduate. We were all graduates of the college, and we kept much of the best of college life in our more matured society. The academic community in those days was emphatically a man's world, full of clubs, free of its time for recreation or exercise, and organized for sport and work, not for love. (It *was* an arid world for women.) We had too, like the undergraduate, a sense of loyalty to our institution which was quite unreasoning, and without relation to the injustices and exploitations of our superiors, which were frequent. Our college was intangibly something quite apart from its president, deans, or heads of departments. They might grind our faces for years on insufficient salaries, exploiting our belief that our duty was to toil for *alma mater*. They might encourage us to think that we would be happy nowhere but at home, then drop us with a sickening crash because we were inbred. They might overwork us in teaching and then break us because we had accomplished too little in scholarship. All this we bitterly resented, without shaking our love and loyalty for the college, which was for us a Platonic absolute. This faith was so irrational that its breakdown later may have been the beginning of a better career for the young scholar; yet while it was strong it gave the academic life a touch of consecration, and bestowed upon it the self-rewarding quality of service in the army or the church. Also, since we were confident of the worth of what we served, even when its agents abused us, we were more easily happy, more generous toward each other, more youthful in our pleasure, than the harder and more skeptical business world outside. The paranoiac temperament was less encouraged in the college than elsewhere. Faith in that somewhat mystical entity, *alma mater*, was an antiseptic for the diseases of egoism.

This was the academic elysium for the contemplative and scholarly mind, the Utopian state within noisy, greedy, full-blooded America. Unfortunately it was a rather old-maidish Utopia, stiff with convention, easily frightened, and disposed always to play safe. Like France of the years following the war, we built our lives upon security.

The economics of security are peculiar. Indeed they have never been studied in this country, where opportunity, until recently, has seemed to wait just around the corner for the active man. We shall know more about the problem in the 1940s than now when the discussion of how to make America safe for those who cannot (note the irony of the old phrase) make money, is just beginning. But security has always been the goal of the teacher and scholar. It is curious that those who debate as to whether men and women can be induced to work without the profit-making motive take so little account of the great population in schools and colleges who even in the last century formed an extensive class that could not, and did not even wish, to *make* money. They could not get rich, and so had to hope for security.

I am not writing economics, and am willing that others should do the deducing from this obvious and neglected fact. But certainly our college community was as dependent upon economic security as the inhabitants of the Soviet republics. For where could our ambitions lead us? Salaries were low, and going lower as the costs of living rose slowly but surely in the first decades of the twentieth century. Promotion was slow. The best the young married man with children could hope for was that his wages would keep pace with his minimum costs. They never did. Always there had to be a supplement—from a private income, from jobs at summer schools which cut into or cut out creative work, from lectures, text books, or an occasional piece of badly paid journalism. The scientist who could rent out his researches did better, but the teachers of the humanities were sorely pressed. And every such dollar earned was a handicap in the race for promotion. Our proper ambition, if we were ambitious, was research; research which consumed endless hours that might bring us fame, but no cash, if indeed we were fortunate enough not to have to pay for our publications. Our success, no matter how resounding, was a success of esteem unless it could be exchanged for an increase in salary. The more money we made in extracurriculum activities, the less we got in in-

creases from the college, which felt that we had
been wasting its time and ours. And if we did
succeed in research, the home authorities were the
last to discover it. Only an offer from some
other college would open their eyes. Therefore,
if one had established a home, one had to risk it.
The best way to stay on in our beloved college
was to threaten to leave it. And that bluff could
be called.

Hence deep down in this pleasant academic
society was a subdued passion, like the peasant's
for his home acres. Our strongest desire was to
be made safe, to stay where we were on a living
wage, to be secure while we worked. It was well
enough to live with ideas, to devote oneself to
vigorous assaults upon the Philistine, but bills
had to be paid, children schooled, the future
made possible for decent living. No scrimping,
no outside earning, could safeguard us. We
were dependent upon the college, which itself
was always pressed for money, and could not
be counted upon to be either judicious or just.

Profit as a motive was bred out of us. We
were frankly ashamed of our petty money-mak-
ings on the side, and inclined to hide them, while
we boasted of our activities in research which

were often far less useful. We quite forgot the
good sense of "All service ranks the same with
God," turning up academic noses at attempts of
our colleagues to succeed in the unacademic. I
remember a friend of mine in the English department who, with a little gift in narrative, and a
nice touch in the essay, wrote decidedly better
(which was not saying much) than most of his
colleagues. He breached the wall of the *Atlantic,*
broke into *Harper's,* published a book that was
called "literary" by the reviewers, and so felt
with some justice that since his job in college
had been teaching how to write, it was to his
credit that he had got himself read by the outside
world in those forms of literature upon which
it was his daily duty to lecture. "It would have
been better," the head of his department was
heard to remark, "that So and So had written
nothing, than what he has written. He should
be doing research." And that was that. The
sin was not the writing per se, but that it was
writing for outsiders, critical, creative writing
not chiefly concerned with the discovery of facts.
And more subtly, that it had been paid for,—not
much to be sure, but still it had been sold to the
populace.

And thus both our needs and our ambition for academic recognition bound us tighter and tighter to a security that only the college could give us. Those who preached the humanities, and they were the backbone of the college, had only one resource. The outside world to them was truly a waste-land where wraiths of broken scholars wandered—no place, no pay, no security. There was fear at their hearts, even the best of them, even those with private fortunes. They felt that they lived on sufferance in the capitalist state.

When I was young it was this hidden fear that impressed me. As I grew older, it was the courage of those who had conquered it—those true scholars, true adventurers in the intellect, who had put the love of security behind them, and who throve upon insecurity. It took a war to teach me that there was no real security anywhere except in the mind,—that if content and safety might be bedfellows, happiness and insecurity could be brothers in arms. Many, most I should say, of the academic community never learned this simple lesson. Their actions, their modes of thought, their lives public and private, were conditioned from beginning to end by the passionate need to be safe.

And that accounts for the timorousness of the academic mind and the persistent note of caution in academic life. Thought was free and speech was reasonably free, and bold men of first-rate capacity used their freedom. Most of us were not bold. We could say what we liked with no immediate penalty, but did not say it. We could do what we liked if our income permitted, but did not do it. Our timidity was emotional.

Radicalism as it exists today was rare in our college. I can remember no instance in which it became a real issue in my time. Why should we have been radical? We knew more of the weaknesses of the capitalist system than did the business world or the proletariat. We knew also very well that we were dependent upon the surpluses of great wealth. Why not? Was there any better way in which they could be spent? Was there any class that worked harder and more disinterestedly than we did for a smaller share of the country's gains? Teaching and research would have to go on under any system, and the experience of those who had been in state universities taught us that our freedom certainly, and our wages probably, would be less if the people paid us. It was not parasitism upon the millionaire that made the historian or social scientiest a restrained and moderate critic. No, he *felt* that way. The unearned increment by the time it got to him was being turned into benefits for society at large. The rich were compensating through him for their exploitations. He was their abbot whose duty it was to transmute thefts into philanthropy. And he was enough of a philosopher to be distrustful of all systems, and particularly skeptical of the blessings of revolution. It was not until the capitalist state showed signs of cracking that the professors became radical. In such matters they were always cautious, but sometimes, certainly, wise.

Their timidity was not so much of the intellect as of the emotions. It was not the great donors they were afraid of, but the conventions of the academic life. The college had become a nest of specialists, each one of which knew only a little but knew that so well that he resented even the interest of an outsider in his subject. Having taught himself with infinite pains to be cautious in handling his facts, he avoided like fire any opinion upon the facts of his neighbor. Conversation became an exchange of dogmatic statement. The humanist knew nothing of science and boasted of his lack of opinion. The scientist kept clear of the humanities and refused to commit himself upon anything that could not be measured. Both declared the philosopher to be an outrageous meddler in other people's pet fields, and waged such successful war that he saved himself from opprobrium by becoming a psychologist. While the curriculum was much debated, there was a gentleman's agreement that the *raison d' être* and relativity of the subjects of instruction should not be argued. They were vested interests. Intellectual curiosity was regarded as a dangerous gift.

How often have I heard a rising faculty discussion collapse like a house of cards when some unfortunate instructor, building a theory upon a deduction, got over his own property line into some specialist's lot, and was brought down in confusion by a blast of facts, which were frequently irrelevant to the argument but had the sacred merit of being specific and unknown except to their possessor. Comparative literature, they used to say, was an exercise for dilettantes, who knew no one literature well enough to talk about it soundly, a true comment, but characteristically narrow in its implications. Wild men they called the deluded who insisted upon seeing education as a whole. For how could anyone see it whole until he had mastered his part? And there was no end to the mastering.

This specialization set the tone of academic discussion. It was another kind of caution which cramped our private lives. We lived in the constant presence of youth and had to preserve our decorum, or thought we had to, even the young ones among us. This may seem amusing, but was not. A professor, like a minister, could never afford to lose his dignity in public, and that in itself was enough to stiffen academic life. He could, curiously enough, be quite rowdy and informal in his classroom, but in the community he must be eminently respectable. He did not want to get drunk. He did not want to frequent brothels. He did not want (or seldom wanted) to elope with his neighbor's wife. But he could not. That was the point. Not even the imagined release of breaking away from the conventions was possible for him, except by straining probability. He could not be anything but a professor in public, and it was dangerous to be anything else in private. Nor was the fact that the academic community was extraordinarily moral very helpful. It never got drunk, swore, fornicated, swindled, never did anything except lie, play politics, and be mean, but these abstentions, whatever might be true for individuals, were obviously artificial for the class. If no professors ran away with other professors' wives, one reason was that they could not afford it. If no professors took part in riots, made incendiary speeches, or fought each other in restaurants, one reason certainly was that if they lost their dignity they were likely to lose their jobs.

All this and much more made a society where public opinion was crystallized. It did not have to be expressed. It was felt, and its sovereignty extended from the dress of college wives to the way one should speak in faculty meeting. It was of this academic opinion that the professor was afraid. It could make or break him quite as easily as his scholarly work and he had to be admittedly a great man to outdare it successfully. There were few rebels. The distinguished scientist whose abominable manners outraged propriety stayed on until he outdid himself by kicking his wife downstairs. But he was wealthy as well as distinguished. The rest of us, who did not wish to kick our wives, yet would have enjoyed a little moral irresponsibility, knew that as wage earners we were overspecialized. There was no job for us outside our caste. We lived in a cautious society, and caution bred timidity. Our intellects were a good deal braver than our emotions.

That is why there was so much that was feminine in academic life, so much jealousy, so much vanity, so much petty intrigue. The faculty seethed with gossip. Some of our best professors were so vain that it was impossible to argue with them over any opinion they had made their own. They would flush at opposition, and were positively ill after an unruly or inattentive class. Not only were individuals jealous of each other, but whole departments. The anthropologists told terrible stories of the vagaries of the geographers, and every scientist believed that the English professors filled their lecture rooms by easy marking. A woman who knows she has no vocation but marriage and the home, and is lost if she loses them, will best understand the timidities, the inhibitions, and the lack of social courage of the professor clinging to his security.

Women, indeed, suffered more than the men

[161]

from the academic atmosphere, though they may have been protected by its relative security. An atmosphere of caution is bad for women, since caution chills the emotions. The college wives did not dress well, because, even when they could afford it, they were afraid of display. The excessive morality of their society suppressed more than their passions. Their duty was to be respectable, and they looked as if they knew it. Born usually in intelligent, well-bred families, their taste was good, but its gratification was increasingly denied them as the needs of a growing family pressed upon income. And that income had no surprises. One could calculate it for years in advance. Their minds were interesting and the triviality which makes so much middle-class American society banal was not their defect. Still, the mixed air of intellectualism and social caution which their husbands breathed was not good for them, or for any female. They looked frigid, whether they were or not. One dares to write so rudely of them because their desiccation was typical not general. The faculty wife who kept her personality and sublimated her emotions into gracious ways and the talk of a free spirit, was one of the finest of American women. She made it possible to say that the academic life in those decades was, in spite of its faults, the most civilized existence which the country at large possessed.

Yet even the best had their trials. Our academic society was made for men and run according to their own tastes, regardless of their womenkind. A faculty dinner party was thus not quite like other dinner parties, although it takes some thinking to discover what made the difference.

The preliminaries were feminine and somewhat flurried, especially if mixed grades of the hierarchy were to be present, assistant professors with full professors, or a dean, or a president. One hostess of my acquaintance solved the problem by entertaining only one rank at a time. The practice was not popular; it was too much like a segregation by races at Ellis Island. The faculty wife had to know something about faculty quarrels, probable promotions, possible dismissals, and as if this were not enough to distract a hostess, in addition, our world being monastic, there was sure to be some crusty old bachelor of importance, who thought children were messy. One young mother dosed hers with aspirin fifteen minutes before the guests' arrival.

Or would it have been soothing syrup in 1910? And then the house! Professors worked at home, hence there were sure to be books everywhere except on the shelves where they belonged, and probably a dictionary or concordance dropped under the dining-room table. And the food and drink? Since everyone knew your salary should it be simpler than necessary in order to suggest plain living and high thinking; or richer than one could afford, in order to flatter the powers who might think that here was a family of taste who did credit to an academic income?

We still escorted the ladies on our arms to the dining room in the early 1900s, with regard for precedence of rank, not age; and once seated there was none of your modern cocktail hilarity, but a weighty pause while we looked about to see who was there. The faculty dinner was not given for pleasure, though it might prove to be pleasurable. It was a duty, as the personnel of the party so clearly indicated. In a compact society such as ours, the satisfaction of choosing for companionship, wit, or beauty was an indulgence seldom permitted. We gave two kinds of dinners:—Informal informal where familiar acquaintances rotated from house to house seeing each other on different sides of many tables. (No public notice was taken of such a dinner.) And informal formal (the purely formal we left to deans and presidents) in which, alas, debts must be paid, heads of departments salaamed to, and new faculty members (who invariably had nervous dyspepsia after their first year) picked off the waiting list. Hence a table as incongruous as the guests of a dining car, and a conversation that too often slid into anecdote or was submerged by a monologue.

But by the salad, a mathematician if he was present, and one usually was, might have noticed the faint, first rise of a curve of interest which was soon to attract wandering talk and focus it so persistently that in spite of the feeble attempts of the hostess the men looked through and soon forgot their partners, until with coffee there was a knot of black coats at one end of the room and a discouraged cloud of skirts at the other. I had seen the same symptoms before in small-town society, but this was different. The men's talk here was not of stocks and business, it was more impassioned, though always bound to the college and its shop. It was gossip, gossip of students, gossip of courses, gossip of the books of scholars, gossip which excluded women from their own province by denying sex except the male, and left them between wind and water, their charm, if any, and there was often much, neglected for the more intoxicating passions of academic life.

It was a bad world for women, but if they came through intact they had learned all the social lessons, could listen to a seventy-year-old celebrity who addressed the ceiling, or talk to a Ph.D. with the milk of his thesis still bubbling on his lips. Alas, many did not come through. To scrimp and be dignified daily throughout the long wait for a professorship, while conscious that the especial gifts of woman were worse than useless without respectability and decorum, chilled the faculty wife, moulded a prim face, and was responsible for a masochistic dowdiness. *Alma mater* was a jealous deity that tolerated no feminism except her own male variety.

Women in the academy society grew salty, eccentric, many-angled in character; or prudish, dry, fussy, and self-indulgent; or, transcending the limitations of their sex, sublimated their difficulties into an amenity of real culture. They

were never passionate—at least in public. But I
have misstated the academic male and the life he
made for himself, if I have implied that he also
was cold, emotionless, far removed from the excitement of the passions. Nothing could be
further from the truth. Outwardly our academe
was cautious in statement and timid in act,
judicious rather than daring, reflective not adven-
turous. And in the inner life, the passions of
sex were controlled, and sometimes atrophied.
But those other passions, ambition, jealousy of
power and place, most of all the passionate hurling of thought and will against the wall of ignorance and through the fogs of obscurantism, and
the endless struggle to think straight and true,
provided emotions enough for any man. In
exact contrast with the rest of America, it was
the intensity of the inner life, the calm of the
outer, which gave to the college a quality which
made it a culture and an experience that was
unique. For men, not women—however it may
have been in the comparatively few colleges
whose faculties were chiefly women.

Why then have the professor and his life been
somewhat of a joke in America? Why has he
been called a "third sex," a lazy dreamer, an un-

practical idealist? Because in the 1900s, when for the first time everybody that was anybody began to go to college, the academic life was an anomaly in the hustle and bustle of a prosperous country on the high road of material progress? Because the professor did not make money, did not drink and wench, did not grab power as power was understood in those days, did not wear himself out at forty, did not (a little later) own a car until his neighbor had two? Because he seemed a nonconformist—what the undergraduates called a "freak"?

These explanations have truth, but leave me skeptical. They are too complimentary to the professor, and too superficial. There was another reason. Something in this pleasant academic life kept the professor as a class from pulling his weight in the community. Perhaps our culture was too young to assimilate the contributions of professional thinkers, especially since they were more interested in thinking than in our culture. Perhaps it was essential (if you believe in a direction for social history) that these college towns should be oases where traditions of long-term thinking and of conserved energy (which some called laziness) should be kept alive while the profit-making system, which seemed to be making the country great, should run its course. Perhaps if the college professor had not persisted in being "unAmerican," there would have been no reserve of disinterested minds for a new era when the motto seems to be "Plan or Bust."

I believe all that, but feel no warmth of pride stirring my memories. We were not in those days holding off for some active future—or certainly most of us were not. We were puzzled idealists trying to keep our footing in two worlds at once. Like the college itself, we had a split personality, and paid for it in being muddled often and sometimes hypocritical. We envied the new-rich progressive country outside our quiet communities, without sufficiently respecting its vital energies, and so acquired the sense of inferiority of those who live in alien civilizations. And this inferiority we tried to conceal, even from ourselves, by an intellectual snobbery which resulted too often in pedantry or pose. Even the English we spoke had an accent of its own. Feeding knowledge to the animals, we were secretly doubtful as to whether it was wisdom, and hid our doubts under a mask of stiff dignity. We younger men

in this difficult decade did become a third sex—
masculine in our resolution to make the life of
the reason keep pace with the instincts, feminine
in our irritabilities, vanities, and our petty
struggles to get that recognition from each other
which the country, with a tolerant smile, quite
emphatically denied us.   In those agreeable academic Edens, scattered all the way from New
England to California, the professor was Adam,
as self-assured and as vain as the original, but
there was the serpent also that kept crawling up
from his uneasy conscience or his hurt pride.   I
leave the professor's wife out of the comparison.
If she played Eve now and then I was too young
to be told about it, but I am sure that the
monastic life she had to share was bad for her
glands.

CHAPTER VII

The Professor

IN A book like this one there is a constant
temptation to play the interpretive philosopher
who explains everything that was in terms of
what happened afterward.   For this a vivid
memory is the best corrective.   I am sure that the
analysis of the preceding chapter is accurate as
far as it goes.   Yet no sooner do I write the last
word of a mode of living that damped the will
while it gave a happy home to the contemplative
mind, than I remember a group of outstanding
professors, pure products of the academic environment, which transcends my definition of
the academic life as a scene where caution and
dignity prevailed while only speculation went
free.   Indeed these men seem to me in retrospect
to have had more character and richer, more
outspoken personalities than their equivalents
among the industrialists and the politicians of

the age.   I wonder if I have been writing nonsense.

It was not nonsense.   Precisely as the tensions and inconsistencies of political life in this same period produced a Theodore Roosevelt, and the opportunities of the business world such unique figures as Carnegie and the elder Morgan, so the struggle between two ideals of living, which was naturally more acute in the colleges than elsewhere, made its own great men. We thought that they were great scholars, but that, for most of them, now begins to seem doubtful.   We believed them to be great thinkers, which, with one possible exception in Sumner, they certainly were not.   But that they were great personalities I am sure; and I believe that they dominated their academic world as in the more efficient machine of the modern university no great teacher does today.   Our gods of the campus were local deities not destined to establish lasting cults, yet they exerted the life-long influence of a divinity that shapes the emotions as well as the mind.   And both undergraduate and young instructor took a proprietary interest in their eminence.   Our attitude toward them was like the relation between the savage and his idols.

We loved them, or hated them, or even despised them, but never escaped from their daily presence in our thoughts. Such men were the justification of the old college. There were never many, sometimes no more than one to a community, but it is of them that the generation shaped by the college still talk.

I shall choose four from my own experience, having discussed several others elsewhere, and without more tiresome analysis try to describe personalities that are important for the young who wish to understand an American society that will be history for them.

The first was a man of mingled sweetness and austerity, mellow in his wisdom, rich in knowledge, yet so thwarted in achievement, so repressed in his life, and dimmed in his ordinary visage, as to be an epitome of all that I have written of the academic life at the turn of the last century. I have seen a photograph of him in a class-book of the sixties, where he appears as a youth dressed in the negligent foppishness of the young litterateur of the bohemian period. And indeed when he began the study and practice of literature, his vocation seemed obvious. That was the afternoon of the age of confidence in the literary art. Professors were still men of letters, lectures were essays (such as Oliver Wendell Holmes wrote), students were gentlemen eager to acquire a genteel style. But Henry Augustin Beers (there must be many who will respond to that name) was not content to be a rhetorician. His idea of scholarship was to know and love all good literature, and all of it he read. I have never mentioned a masterpiece in any language that he had not been through, and from which he could not quote; nor a poem or story of merit, even if obscure, in our own American literature that was not fresh with all the context of its times in his memory. For him Milton was as much alive as Emerson, whom he had known. His arguments were not of date and source (though he was accurate and far-seeing), but of matters of blood and brain and sex, and of neighbors, accidents, temperament, and sheer aptitude, which explain what is both important and explicable in the background of art. Yet his mind, though so stocked, was never a specialist's. He was an amateur in military history, a connoisseur in acting, especially women's acting, though he could seldom afford the theatre, and he knew in a Connecticut meadow where the gentian grew and on a hillside pasture where to plant the pine.

He seemed an old man when I first knew him well, in 1900. Bent over his desk, reading with difficulty from frayed note sheets in a husky voice, he would pause at intervals to goggle through thick lenses at his inattentive class while he asked a perfunctory question, sometimes not waiting for an answer. "Old Beers" they called him, with a surprised affection for so musty a creature, from whose lips between the crash and jangle of trolley cars outside a sentence now and then was audible of such pith and beauty that lazy fingers began to scribble in the notebooks.

After class some of us would linger until the routine was over, then draw near his desk with questions. Slowly the drooped head would lift, the sensitive fingers begin to smooth his limp moustache, the eyes behind the thick spectacles would light and twinkle, the voice grow mellow; and then, if our opening was fortunate, his real teaching would begin. He had a mind that was skeptical, humorous, affectionate, an impeccable taste, a humanity so deep and so cultivated that as he talked civilizations took color, authors became men, and poetry was felt to be that rhythm of personal experience which Robert Frost defines, and which Beers of all the critics I have known most infallibly could bring back from the past.

Here was a man sure of his loves and hates, who questioned the validity of good thought and beauty as little as love or food. He did not preach culture but was the thing itself. He had not acquired knowledge as a tool but because his mind desired it. Where his colleagues knew about literature, he knew literature itself, and more about it that was relevant than the most erudite. His mind was encyclopedic, but it was a commentary not a reference book. Other scholars knew what idyll of Theocritus was a source for "Lycidas," he could tell why Milton read it and what he had done with his reading. The college knew, or thought it knew, why literature should be taught, and what should be taught of it. Beers was himself an example of that rebirth in literature which gives margins to the imagination. No one knowing him could doubt the efficacy of the humanities. And it was significant in that atmosphere of jealousy of science and the new technologies, that there, too, his interests were keen.

The Professor

Yet it would be too much to say that Henry Beers had a successful life. Burdened with many dependents upon an income whose real value had steadily shrunk, he was deprived of all those recreations which minds like his are made to enjoy. A reader of European literature, his only trip abroad was made in his youth. Society had to come to him, for he was too poor to go to society. I do not suppose that in twenty years he made as many journeys, even of a day, to New York and Boston. In his own college town he was a hermit, living in an unfashionable suburb, hidden away among his books. On our quiet campus, his bent frame, his worn clothes, his shy and inward air as he shuffled from his class-room toward the library, were like a survival of a more pinched and austere age. Freshmen stopped to wonder as he passed. He was young in heart and the richness of his inner life must have been some compensation for the poverty of his experience. Yet he was a defeated man.

It was not his restricted means or his weight of personal responsibility that bore him down. They were the agents of his defeat, but the cause was the new utilitarianism of the campus. I do not mean the romantic materialism of the undergraduates which young instructors were vainly fighting. Beers was too intelligent and too familiar with the history of his own country not to have understood better than we the reasons for their Philistinism, and too true a humanist not to have stood up against it unbowed. Indeed, in spite of his defeatism, he became a legend among the students because of the evident sincerity of his culture. It was the demands of his own colleagues that put the mask on his face, and drove his vision inward. In his youth a professor of English was expected to be a maker as well as a teacher of literature. Much amateur creativeness of a genteel kind had resulted. But Beers was neither an amateur nor genteel. He was a poet of sorts, a prose writer of excellent skill. He deserved the name of man of letters. It is not surprising, therefore, that the demand for science in the study of literature caught him unprepared. He was a reader of literature not a collector of facts about it, although in accurate information he had few rivals. Nevertheless his methods were not the methods of natural science. It was conclusions, not data, that seemed to him important. He was, I believe, planning to write the literary history of America which has not yet been properly written, when philology as the Germans understood it came into fashion. There was a sudden cry for medievalists, phoneticians, and practitioners of exact research, with no literary nonsense about them. Those areas of literary history which were difficult because of their remoteness, and obscure because their poverty in artistic worth had repelled earlier readers, became the cynosures of scholarship. Anyone could write of Tennyson or Browning, but it took scholarship to discuss the "Andreas" or "Handlyng Synne."

In the flurry, a comprehensive knowledge of all good English literature and a minute familiarity with American writing seemed of little price. Men were brought to teach what he was supposed not to know. His own classmates (I speak from knowledge) began to regard him as an old-fashioned putterer in outworn themes, who might at any moment publish the poetry he was known to write. His contributions already made to the history and criticism of American literature were compared unfavorably with research in the much harder history of Anglo-Saxon, his charming essays upon life in an earlier Yale were regarded as conclusive evidence against his aptitude for scholarship. And his inefficiency as a teacher of the massed young of an unliterary period put the last nail in the coffin of his reputation. In self-defense he published two books based upon a thorough investigation of romanticism, a subject then fashionable. They are still standard, but his heart was not in them. They were neither literature, of which he was capable, nor criticism of that American field where he was without a peer, but which in that day of excessive reverence for European scholarship was felt to be too trivial for a serious mind that should be engaged in establishing the authorship of a bad pseudo-Shakesperian play. When I first knew him he was already listed as a liability from the past.

His old age knew a brief sunset. He lived long enough to see a respect for literature as such appear again in the colleges, though not quite long enough to witness (with what an ironic smile!) the droves of prospective Ph.D.s turned from the exhausted veins of English literature to dig in the American soil, rediscovering often what he long since had known, but knowing so much less well what it meant and what to do with it! Before he died his house was a place of pilgrimage.

The Professor

It was the times that destroyed him. The college was unsure of its own ends, uncertain of the value of the humanities, yet honorably unable to yield to the hearty materialism of the times. Compromising between rigid discipline and the romance of college life, it distrusted instinctively a man whose culture was homogeneous and of a kind that its half-way measures could never produce. If Beers had stiffened his backbone instead of withdrawing into the city of his mind, he might have been our leader. If he had been a more powerful teacher, a more self-assured scholar, he would have made it necessary to respect him. But he was not aggressive. Unfortunately those with access to the inner light of the humanities seldom are, nor are their minds the stuff out of which missionaries are made. It is too bad, for what we get from the missionaries of culture proves so often not to be the Gospel! Yet no lover of literature went out of college in my day untouched by his influence.

My second example was also a professor of English, but of a breed so different that I am left wondering whether the rich university of today can show such diverse egoes. He was a bearded man, short, catlike on his feet, with a shifty eye and a quick tread across the campus that seemed always to conceal a limp. Professor Albert S. Cook was a finished product of the German philological mill, who had been brought to the university to introduce methodology—how he rolled the word on his tongue!—into our somewhat haphazard graduate school of language and literature. He had already made a reputation in Anglo-Saxon philology, indeed his first-year book in that language was a model of its kind. He brought the gospel of science in literary studies.

No man in my day was more unpopular with the faculty and the few undergraduates that came under him, more worshipped by a small circle of devotees. He was, indeed, in our clubable community the exact counterpart of the grind and freak among the undergraduates. Not that he worked harder than his colleagues or produced more. But instead of the lazy lecture, oft used if excellent, which was the fare of our advanced courses, he offered a battle, incalculable from the moment of beginning, impromptu, unfair from every college viewpoint, since it was impossible to guard one's weaknesses or listen to a conventional lecture with an easy mind. And, like the grind, he had an indifference amounting to contempt for the amenities of our academic living. Indeed there was something sadistic about the man, a by-product of his intensities, which accounted in part for both the dislike and for the slavish devotion that he inspired, although the deeper cause of his unpopularity was by no means so creditable to his enemies. I have seen him reduce a woman graduate student to tears, and seem to enjoy it. Of men he was afraid. If they yielded to his intellectual dominance he would work for their advancement, but let them waver in their admiration and the knife in a second would sever the umbilical cord. You were either *his* student, or someone else's, and if someone else's, beware! No mercy, no help. Indeed here was a perfect example of the feminine male, in whom a masculine intellect operated with all the vanity, jealousy, pettiness, and infinite subtlety of a woman.

A fine philologist, his mind was nevertheless too scattering and too prone to quick generalizations for sustained scholarship. Like the scientists of the day, his work was contained in brief papers recording discoveries, many of them minute, if not trivial. Unfortunately they were not steps in the study of the nature of light or the weight of the atom, but rather chips of literary history, the date of a Northumbrian cross, the classic parallels to a line in Milton. In such a strictly limited field as the teaching of elementary Anglo-Saxon he was admirable; and among all my teachers in that day he alone seemed interested in the relations between the categories of knowledge, in one terse sentence throwing more light on the proper development of a project in research than came from all the rest of the faculty.

But the college and its closely related graduate school encouraged his weakness rather than his strength. He knew little of literature as litera-ture, though much of its history, little of esthetics, and nothing that was original of philosophy. Yet it was these that he taught us instead of his proper subject, which was philology. The top dressing of smug culture on the crude vigorous soil of American life was a stench in his nostrils. He felt a call to convert the heathen, to smite the Philistines. He hurled the middle ages at our head—*his* middle ages, not always the genuine article. He challenged us with masterpieces. He talked now of Beethoven, now of Aeschylus. If we mentioned Horace, he made us translate him.

[184]

If we spoke of religion, he made us define our terms. No gentleman's agreement as to required knowledge stood for a moment with him. He demeaned himself so far as to nag women with general questions that it is certain he could not have answered satisfactorily himself. He aroused hate and a fierce opposition. He burned through our bourgeois laissez-faire, and set us searching for the principles upon which we lived and which we were willing to defend. He was a great teacher, if to be a great teacher is to set the mind afire, the greatest I have ever known.

But not a wise one. The college asked him for linguistics but what he tried to give it was something it badly needed, a philosophy of esthetics, a philosophy of literature. And for this he was willing but inapt and unprepared. His taste was defective, his knowledge of art entirely theoretical, his feeling for literature that of an intuitive but inexperienced woman. Having read for methodology, he had built up his cloudy theories upon hearsay and platitude. It took me years to break away from his vicious methods of criticism, vicious because they began with a theory and never got beyond the literal meaning of the text. He could relate a symphony of Mozart to a comedy of Congreve without really knowing what the first was made of or the second about. There was more literature in Beers's little finger than in Cook's lifetime, though for the college at large it stayed in his little finger. Cook broke up our minds, sneered at us, bullied us, threw absurd generalizations at our heads, tripped us on trivialities, taught his women to talk solemn nonsense without knowing that it was nonsense, wrapped his own esthetic ignorance in words, and made us angry, and thus alive. If Beers was a belated humanist, he was a schoolman come from the Middle Ages, playing with science and literature instead of theology. And indeed it may be said of him as of many great medieval scholastics that he was a great teacher who was usually wrong.

Inevitably our college faculty with its genteel reserves, its mingled contempt and fear of the raw competition outside, its defeatism and indifferentism, would get sooner or later such a crabbed spirit who struck blows for the sake of hurting, and tried to make us all into what he supposed was the image of an Athenian. Yet it did us good. He was the whip with the nasty undercut of my education.

The Professor

For the third of my figures from these now so distant nineties and first nineteen hundreds, I will turn to science as science was understood then.

I wish I could recreate in words William H. Brewer. He was a vast, shambling man, with the face of an old ram stretched on the drum of a great head, a ragged beard that never covered a spreading goiter, and a squeaky voice that seemed to come from some observer sitting inside. Indeed his whole life had been concentrated on observation, and I do not believe that his imagination was ever actually in the lecture room, but rather on the deck of a sinking ship in the Arctic, or following the wild camels of Arizona, or noting the geography of the Sierras, which he explored, and where there is a great snow-based peak that bears his name. In his lectures, except for brief moments of awareness when he would show on his chart that the ancestry of some disturber on the rear seat ran back to the wild ass of the deserts, he was shadow boxing. His subject, I suppose, was evolution; to this day I do not know what he was supposed to teach, so widely did his lectures range; but more and more as the year went on his discourse narrowed to a fierce controversy with an absent antagonist, the great German biologist Weismann, who had foully disposed of Brewer's pet theory of the inheritance of acquired characteristics, by experiments that our professor asserted to be inconclusive, insufficient, and probably fraudulent. Again and again while we sat in boredom or fascination according to our sense for drama, the squeaky voice would rise, the broad face flush, the class-room fade from his consciousness, while with a lance-like pointer he stabbed at his visionary antagonist, and crumbled him at last with his other hand into broken bits of chalk.

We got evolution from him certainly, and useful tips on horse races, for he was an expert in breeding and predicted the two-minute trotter within five years of its actual appearance. (He shocked the college town also by subscribing for all the racing papers.) We got glimpses of the passion and the confidence of science in a day when it seemed that all wisdom as well as all knowledge was to be its province. Nevertheless, most of his squeaky eloquence drifted over our unruffled heads, so that now his classes remember only that he pronounced "Injun" in the old American manner, and "cigarettees" in his own peculiar fashion, leaving them certain of evolution but doubtful of what it was or how it came about. I am sorry that we let our thoughts wander, for we were watching a tragedy, and hearing a parable more truly significant for our generation than the soon-to-be-disproved physics and economics we were being taught in other classrooms. Here, indeed, was the parallel to the industrial profit-making life from which most of us had come. Here was science, unrelated to the rest of life (except horse racing), yet cocksure and triumphant, announcing multitudes of observations collected with incredible energy, which were to reveal the Great Secret at last. No end to the amassing of scientific fact—tails of monkeys, customs of the anthropoids, the results of mixed marriages, statistics of venereal diseases, the lifting power of flood waters, the ancestry of the bull dog. Precisely as the new industrialists were piling up millions in their greed for power, which when gained they gave away or used to make new millions, so this robber baron of science took toll of everything that came his way and stored his loot upon innumerable note sheets. In contrast to the tight little disciplines of our curriculum, he offered us the world

—as he saw the world. But alas, it was all un-controlled experiment, the infinite details of which slid over our minds, leaving us as incapable of realizing the real significance of the growing complexity of civilization as were our fathers who had been trained in the classics. There was dynamite in Brewer's course, but no caps to set it off. He was content to make us wonder at the tricks nature could play. I am unjust, for doubtless many a man of our time was prepared by that prelude to natural science to respect (or fear) the scientist when later he began to attack our reckless exploitation of resources of wealth and humanity. Yet Brewer saw only an age of miracle where every rock and toad and gutter had its story, which to know was to understand.

After his death I had occasion to go into his study. It was a capacious room, its walls hidden by box upon box of notes, while from the ceiling a dozen baskets hung on pulleys, each overflowing with records and documents. A lifetime of observation! And they were all to be burnt! Nothing had been deduced from them that affected thinking; no man would undertake to go through them; their utility had been only the delight of observation, and what increase in knowledge his contemporaries had gained. I saw an equivalent sight twenty years later when a strong box was opened in the 30s. There were the accumulated profits of a capitalist lifetime, all paper and most of it worthless. Brewer was a man true to his time, true to a college that was not sure of what it wanted. Yet he was a personality that, as I recall him, makes me wish to write only in praise. Whatever he said and did, he himself was an education.

I shall close this chapter with one more scientist, whose science was above reproach, since, although its fundamental tenets have been upset since his day, they have been changed by such methods of thought and experiment as he himself taught. The physical theory he gave us proved much of it to be wrong, and indeed his was not the highly original mind to set it right, but he had the true scientific attitude, which is neither possessive nor dogmatic. He taught us not to wonder, but to reason.

Yet it was not his science that brings him to memory here. The best physics in the world would never have stirred my imagination in those days, unless freed from its husk of mathematics. It was his solution of a common college problem. He alone among all my teachers faced our Philistine ideas of high-brow nonsense, and faced them down. Charles S. Hastings was a man of some elegance, whose pince-nez held between finger and thumb was no more delicately balanced than his enunciation of an admirable English. He told no stories, embroidered upon his subject no references to undergraduate life, made no colloquial concessions to the unintellectual. If it was a dynamo he was explaining, or the conservation of energy, he kept to his theme, but to that theme he gave the skill in composition, the nicety of expression, and the urbanity of a great painter. Language for him was a garment whose every fold and shade was conditioned by the infinite complexity of truth. An artist in words, he used them not as words merely but as the only medium by which a thought world alien to us could be interpreted to minds that feebly but inevitably responded. It was a culture, yet not culture as we thought of culture, for the substance of his discourse was practical, inescapable fact (and yet not fact but hypothesis so he told us), such fact as business men and engineers dealt with, and hence part of the experience that our home town regarded as reality. And yet this

tangible reality became on his tongue so subtle, so evidently related to ends that no immediate application could satisfy, that in spite of ourselves we became aware of the nature of the search for truth in a region where neither sentiment nor platitude would avail.

He tricked us. The physics he taught we hated and learned badly; the philosophy remained. For here was the sense of form, the devotion to abstract ends, which our college life repudiated, in a hard-boiled subject that could not be bluffed. He tricked himself, too, I suspect, since his private passion was literature, and it was he who, long before the litterateurs discovered him, introduced me to the passionate metaphysics of Herman Melville. The ploughing in of formula and experiment he left to his subordinates. What he gave us himself was a pattern of exquisite thinking and an idea which we dimly apprehended that all truth must ultimately be beautiful. And also, on a lower level —but what a lesson for barbarians!—that cold facts could best be imparted in the courtesy of perfect English admirably spoken. Even the bums and the roughnecks were orderly in his class.

CHAPTER VIII

Scholars and Scholarship

$\mathcal{T}$HE four professors of the last chapter were
living instances of the dominance of personality
in the Gothic Age of the American college. Two
of them were scientists, two humanists. While
the scientists were completely self-expressive, the
humanists were frustrate scholars who never
attained their ends. This contrast was no accident.

Brewer, although his collected works were
only a million note sheets, now ashes, fulfilled
his intellectual destiny. He was of the race of
explorers, men searching passionately for a river,
a city, or a missing link that proves to be illusion,
men whose maps are wrong, whose specimens are
ill-assorted, yet they cross new passes and track-
less deserts, opening trails for the better disciplined minds that follow. His mountain in
the Sierras is precisely the monument that he
would have desired. Not so with the humanists

of the Gothic Age, the workers in history and particularly in literature, too many of whom were somewhat tragic figures, with divided minds. One word was always on their tongues —scholarship, a term to which no two of them gave exactly the same definition. Indeed they served a two-faced god.

The scholar's passion in the college of that day was for knowledge. His enthusiasm was well warmed, if not always well lit, by a burning desire to get the facts. When, just out of college ourselves, we first sat in something like intimacy under old teachers who now proposed to make teachers of us, what they taught us first was to despise the cultivated amateurs who in the last generation had lectured upon the amenities of history and literature. Lowell, whose critical essays were rich in opinions but short in facts, was held up to scorn. Longfellow was mentioned also, with a shrug,—a professor who did translations. Accuracy in little things was the new virtue, and we were encouraged to believe that the world was more in need of correct texts, exact dates, and a knowledge of sources, than of estimates, appreciations, and opinions which, however just, were not scientific because they could not be proved. Browning's grammarian had given the slogan,—

This man decided not to Live but Know—

a line which was often quoted. Since an accurate text of a masterpiece was a necessary preliminary to a correct interpretation, insensibly the establishing of the text began to seem more important than an appreciation of the work; and, naturally, the more corrupt or the more difficult the text, the more merit there was in studying it. For great works of literary art belonging to a past era, where every resource of history had to be exhausted in order merely to understand, this obsession with knowledge gave great results. Chaucer and Dante came to life again in this age of scientific scholarship. Yet too often the scholar could tell you everything about a poem except why it was poetry.

The classicists, and the teachers of modern literature who were heirs to their dictatorship of culture, had dubiously and with unconcealed condescension given to pure science a minor place in the curriculum. Now the scientific approach became fashionable. Scholars in literature who called themselves scientific began to dominate the graduate schools and extend their influence into the sacred precincts of the undergraduate college. Applying the technique of scientific research to language, they revealed an evolution with laws of its own the discovery of which was a noble extension of knowledge. Then they moved from linguistics into literary history and soon were re-writing the vague and impressionistic chronicles of our literary past, substituting exact tests of dialect, allusion, and rhythm for the guesswork of earlier historians. The bastard works fathered upon Chaucer and Shakespeare were given right-ful parents or put upon the town, and indebted-ness to tradition or to environment was rightly indicated.

But neither literature nor history is explained by the facts of its origin or its background. The historian at best gives a personal interpretation. The scientific researcher at the most provides the essential facts. And the poet or novelist, espe-cially, has created a new world which absorbs his observations into a whole that is by no means only a sum of its parts.

> *Nothing of him that doth fade,*
> *But doth suffer a sea-change*
> *Into something rich and strange.*

The scientific impulse in literary scholarship was indifferent to such nice metamorphoses of subject matter. It sought facts where facts could be found and its disciples soon began to see all written records as a quarry in which the mysterious nature of a crystal could be ascertained by the same chemical analysis that demonstrated the composition of a block of limestone to be $CaCO_3$.

Envy was partly responsible for this singular warping of judgment. The humanist scholars of my youthful day were jealous of the great achievements of natural science. Science had begun to turn away resolutely from the "wonders of nature" which had fascinated men like Brewer, and with specks of dirt microscopically considered, or drops of fluid in a test tube, or glacial scratches on a stone, was making discoveries of stupendous importance. In my own university before my day research men in "stinks" and other utilitarianisms had been tolerated but kept in a social position definitely inferior to the humanists, so that when Harvard asked for representatives from Yale at her two hundred and fiftieth anniversary, no professors from the new Scientific School were included in the list drawn up by our President.　Now science was having its revenge.

Scientists in the college of the 1900s were still regarded as socially dubious by the wives of classicists and English professors, but the husbands of these social leaders of the college had, without being fully aware of it, become imitators of what they had so lately disdained.　If boulders the ploughman turned up in the fields and mice infected by disease held secrets valuable to man, why should not the bypaths and deserts and unexplored areas of literary history be as rewarding to researchers?　And so began that race after the obscure, the difficult, and the neglected which, yielding rich spoils where science was the proper tool, led elsewhere to the vast accumulations of unimportant facts about literary history which clog the shelves of libraries and whiten the hair of the modern historian, who cannot write a page without consulting a shelf-full of pamphlets, many of which cancel each other.　The parallel with the world outside, where technological advance was accompanied by a senseless race for self-defeating power and by riches badly used, is too obvious to need pointing.

Both sets of competitors—the millionaires

and the literary scholars—failed to define their ends; neither, as a rule, knew what to do with their prizes when they got them. But there was this difference, that while out in the world everyone appreciated the value of money, the undergraduates for whom the college had been made, their parents, and the alumni, were quite unable to comprehend the passion of the scholar who spent his life in clearing up a text, leaving the study of literature as such to lesser men, or to the next generation.

For the true scientist in history and literature, without whose work history, criticism, and interpretation are alike difficult, if not impossible, I have the greatest respect. But alas, few of us in those days were scientists by nature, but rather young men in love with books; and even if our minds had been scientific there would not have been room for us all in the regions of literary history still unexplored! These two obvious facts did not weigh for a moment with our superiors. They had seen the Chaucer canon made, and the border ballads rescued from oblivion. So they urged us on to tasks which inevitably were of lesser importance. Ambition and research became synonymous words. Literature—our reading—we might pick up in odd hours—our work, our future lay in literary history, in discovery, in new facts. Many a critic and poet was broken on the wheel. Many an able intellect, confronted with the job of classifying the paragraph endings in Cicero, left scholarship for the law or business where hard work could bring him at least a good income. The born investigators among us found themselves in a golden age where the dating of a miracle play might bring a professorship to a youngster whose critical estimates of great prose or poetry were as unformed as an undergraduate's. The rest were driven and harried.

And so we all went in for literary history, except those favored few with a fortunate talent for linguistics, which was a true science and so yielded its secrets to the investigator. Human nature being what it is, we naturally sought for new literary history where no Taines or Saintsburys had been mightily exploring before us. It was Cynewulf not Shakespeare that we dug into, the romances of chivalry rather than Racine, and Goethe's borrowings from the Arabic instead of an interpretation of the second part of Faust.

Some of it was useful, much of it seems a little

absurd now; but if anyone doubts the influence of this Alexandrianism let him read the list of thesis subjects in the humanities, even today, remembering how many tens of thousands of college youths have been taught their literature by men and women whose most active preparation was in a method of research (usually sound) expended upon a subject which was often not worth investigating. There went the laborious days—and the odd hours were left for the reading and study of masterpieces. For they all knew that appointment and promotion in the humanities came as a result of research, and the shrewder were well aware that the best jobs (in English at least) came out of the eighth to the fifteenth centuries.

It was the cross-word puzzle age of scholarship. The myriad intelligent minds among the populace who spend their hours over puzzles today, are amateurs in a job which these scholars made professional. The cross-word puzzle is research reduced to an absurdity in which no end is proposed except the satisfaction of an occupied mind seeking a solution which answers nothing but the desire to find whatever was hid. Great scholars, as Chaucer reminds us, are not always

[203]

the wisest men; indeed they are much like other
men in their impulses, and in those days it is certain that many of them were puzzle-minded.
And many of their students came to believe that
solving a puzzle was the essence of the study of
literature. For research is the best of all puzzles
because the most difficult. Nor is it surprising
that when science by fitting together the broken
pieces of the earth's history gave us a new history
of man, the humanists should also get to work
with their books and pencils, forgetting sometimes to estimate the value of what they sought
in the pleasure of the seeking. I knew a so-called
fabulist in my days in the graduate school, who
for years had compared manuscript with manuscript of the fables of Aesop, tracing their indebt-
edness one to another by the use of "wolf" for
"fox" or a peculiarity in the ass that wore the
lion's skin, until he had curves of dates and influences running clear across the European Middle Ages. It all meant nothing. The last fable
was substantially the same as the first, for they
were all copyist's work with not a touch of creativeness in the whole series. Indeed he was careful to leave out the elaborate reworkings of the
old stones in the so-called beast epic, as corrupt

[204]

versions adulterated by the egoism of a creative artist. It meant no more than counting the bricks in a hundred city blocks. Yet he was a happy man. His task extended onward indefinitely. He would never finish, and so need never draw conclusions. He had a puzzle so good that it got him a professorship. The case was extreme, yet illuminating.

And all this was going on in the midst of the ardent college life of the Gothic Age with its romantic materialism and its distrust of whatever made one stop and think. While we were busy with this puzzle-book scholarship the need of the student for the gospel of sweetness and light went often by default. We were in truth kept so busy on Old French, phonetics, and methodology that it was left to our naive minds to discover what literature itself really was, and how to teach it.

In moments of relaxation between research in the library and the teaching of a class of Freshmen I used to ask myself what was the study of literature. Even as a child I had been puzzled by conflicting ideas of knowledge. When I was an ardent collector of minerals, an old scientist told me, "It isn't the beautiful crystal of quartz or of fluorite or of beryl that is important; it is the rare and ugly diaspore, the greasy pseudomorph, the dull stone that points toward a new species." Even to my boyish mind this seemed a hard doctrine. For it was not because the crystal was rare, but because it was beautiful that I wished to possess it. The hexagonal of quartz had attained a perfection in which the lumpish columbite had failed.

I remembered this when I began to think about the teaching and study of prose and poetry. Sufficient for our masters in the Gothic Age was the study of literary history which supplied them with problems enough and material for endless teaching. Milton's "Lycidas" attacked, worried, dissected, and put together again, would keep them busy for a week.

Yet evidently this was only a preparation for the study of literature. One needed philosophy, since so much prose and poetry was difficult to understand without experience in the schools of philosophic thinking. There was psychology, which got its best illustrations, outside the laboratory, in fiction. There was religion, love, esthetics, all germane to literature. There were the complex ramifications of social history that determine the accent of a literary age. There was the continuity of human experience, highly important, since the relation of a book to this continuum seems to be the one criterion by which we can test the greatness of a literary masterpiece. Nor should it be forgotten that unless the teacher can integrate the literature of the past with the living mind before him, the literature he teaches stays dead.

There was plenty for us to do, but no one— or only a Beers here and there, and he inarticulately, by example—told us how much. Rather, we were urged to specialize. Our teachers, having discovered by their own investigations how frequently their predecessors had been wrong in fact or date, were determined that neither they nor we should overstep the line of exact knowledge. Get the first thing first, which was the facts. Let the rest wait—do it after hours— read in the summer—fill up the gaps later;—if you wish to be promoted contribute now to exact knowledge, not of literature, which is too vague a term to mean anything for a specialist, but of the facts about literature. And since, unfortunately, and in sharp contrast to natural science, the most important facts are known, wade in after the unimportant. To this, in our feeble hands, the study of literature came down in the first decades of the twentieth century. No wonder that we were ignorant and often contemptuous of the writers of our own time. I remember the chivalrous revolt of the male students when a hard-working woman in our graduate school was denied her degree because in an oral examination it was discovered that she had never heard of Oscar Wilde and never read Thomas Hardy. What chance had she, with her brain sunk a fathom deep for three years in the fifteenth century! And since we youngsters of the period were already beginning to take on the literary education of the new generation of students, it is not surprising that, aiming to make specialists like ourselves of our classes, we often failed to persuade them to enjoy the most likable books. Is this the reason that the American college graduate, especially the male graduate, unlike the educated class of any other great nation, is not a reader of books, especially of books in that field of belles lettres which he most frequently elected to study in his student days? He got the facts, and, like his instructors, let the culture wait for a better opportunity, which, as the sales of good books in the United States pathetically show, has not yet come.

I do not forget the great teachers who broke through these conventions of scholarship, and the great scholars (fewer in number) who made use of their own researches to illumine the intricate nature of literature itself. And I am aware that the ideal of literary study I have described lies beyond the power of one man to achieve in a lifetime. He cannot accurately know all he should know, and if he guesses he is no longer scientific. But this is true even of mathematics. Push far enough and you are involved in the complex of life itself, in which yesterday's dinner or today's contact with an idea has implications involving the outermost star. Yet surely of all the professions the study of philosophy and the study of literature and the study of history most require a flexible, intuitive mind, aware that neither a lyric, nor a moral axiom, nor the fate of a nation, can be disposed of finally without determining the business of the universe. And surely in such professions the willingness to link fact with fact, and where there are no facts to point the way of conjecture and interpretation, is infinitely important. In literature especially, which deals essentially with the concrete expression of emotion and thought, intuition, especially if it is based on a rich experience, should begin its work while the returns are still coming in from scientific research, and continue long after the last fact is run down. I fear that the specialist scholars of the Gothic Age who were not also great personalities, gave us too little of their own selves, of which indeed they often knew much less than of grammar or mythology. They left out the middle term of teaching—which is man the interpreter and the interpreted. Shelley seemed safest to them when studied as a by-product of the romantic movement, and Shakespeare's bawdry most examinable in terms of the laxities of the Renaissance. No reputable scientist (they thought) would exercise his intuitions upon the retreat of a glacier; nor would they upon a sonnet.

And so many a scholar in our college, which still relied upon the humanities for the core of education, became an intellectual spinster. Like spinsters, he had suppressed some of his vital functions, and narrowed the outlet for his energies. He was afraid of everything he had not investigated, and hence his work grew more and more remote from life. And like some spinsters he met with an incomprehension hard to bear. His students were also working tirelessly for ends that no philosopher would have approved. They specialized in athletics precisely as he specialized in the emendation of texts. But their objectives were easily comprehensible to the country at large and hence to themselves. Their rewards of college fame or social position were immediate, and popular opinion approved of them. But the scholar's ideal was the perfect knowledge which precedes all wisdom. And its visible evidence was to be seen in books which only his colleagues could read, and which indeed represented only fragments of imperfect knowledge, of whose ultimate use he himself seemed scarcely aware. Thus students of the college and the public alike, could see in scholarship only something that was eccentric, futile, unAmerican, which could not be taken seriously by red-blooded men. The gulf between those who wished to know and those who wished to do was not bridged by such misapprehensions. Did the scholars wish to bridge it? Certainly in the product of the humanistic scholarship of those decades there was very little upon which a grow-ing civilization could be nourished.

I apologize for this excursion into criticism. It is not irrelevant because it helps to explain what has so often puzzled me, the defeatism and timorousness of the college, which were so often accompanied by sporadic displays of magnificent courage and commanding personality. There was, I am sure, lurking in the professor's heart an uneasy sense that the research by which his colleagues judged him was not really important. He knew that his ordering of Shakespeare's son-nets or his analysis of the subjunctive in Anglo-Saxon, was a permanent contribution, however slight, to the fund of human knowledge, more permanent, if less immediately useful, than a fac-tory or a lawsuit. Yet he knew also that to the country, and to his students, his work seemed to be an eccentricity of a belated adolescent, who played twenty questions while life roared past outside his study window. Remembering Mary and Martha, he wondered whether his dutiful service in the kitchen of literature would be pro-perly appreciated, even by the Deity. It was after such moments of painful introspection that he would close his books, and with a grim resolve to make himself felt in his generation, charge into his classroom, and grapple with the callow imagination of his pupils, until even their conventional minds were ploughed up and planted here and there with distrust of their own smugness. Thus great teachers might be made.

The outcome was not usually so spectacular. Some men swung the broad axe in the forest of obscurity, determined to make a clearing where light would shine. They were the Gummeres, Kittredges, Lounsburys, Furnesses, who gave our scholarship distinction. But the scholar of the Gothic Age was more often warped than exalted. He had lost the simple confidence of the monk in the efficacy of his beads and masses, without acquiring the hearty assurance of the layman. His eyes saw the steep and rocky road to truth, his ears heard public opinion whirring past on a cement highway. And he did queer things.

An able philologist spent his later years in literally hurling morsels of erudition at the outside world (which never read them), nodules so inconsiderable and yet so tough as to amaze the observers who knew his power over a wide range of scholarship. He had become a boy again, throwing stones at his indifferent enemies. A source of a source of a source of a great poem, he seemed to say, is more important than your turmoil of love, hate, and possessing. Another, who died frustrate in middle age, leaving behind him a tradition of subtle and penetrating lecturing upon literature, had his heart set upon poetry not scholarship. In the critical academic atmosphere his slender talent withered. His lectures, shot through with melancholy, were the byproducts of a defeated imagination. Still another scholar, finding that he had nothing in particular to say about what he studied, set himself to read by measure, his ambition, in which he succeeded, being to read through all extant Old French literature before he was sixty, making notes as he went on curiosities of grammar and vocabulary. He would announce with glee each month his current mileage.

But the most interesting instance by far of this college complex was Lounsbury, whom I have mentioned in early chapters. Here was vigor of mind and vigor of personality such as it would have been hard to find more richly blended elsewhere in America. He fought through four years of the Civil War, emerging with an undying hatred for the intellectual deadness of the military life. He wrote in his youth three or four novels which no one would publish, and closed that chapter with hearty contempt for all incompetents who dabbled in the making of literature. Then he set out on the road to scholarship, and was brilliantly successful. He wrote a definitive book on Chaucer, and having got a name, began, like our own generation of youths whose minds were wounded in the war, to satisfy his grudge against human stupidity. His specialty was to expose the folly of scholars and critics of the past. No pedantry of grammarians was too ancient for his scorn. With wit and satire he stirred up the dust in the lumber rooms of scholarship, banging the heads of nonentities against their own books. And while he had little feeling for beauty and less for emotion, he so reverenced the fine mind finely articulate that he made most of the greatest English literature his own by heart. I have heard him recite Dryden and Chaucer by the hour without a book.

In earlier periods and with a different erudition, his fame would have been national. In the English eighteenth century, as a classicist, he could not have escaped high distinction. But the prestige of the classics had waned, and no substitute like English literature could rival the lost dominance of Latin and Greek over popular respect. Lounsbury was just a professor of English, who, except among his fellow scholars, had only a local reputation.

Does this explain the fury with which he fell upon the dumb undergraduate? The lightnings of his wrath which played about his books, burnt out in a vacuum. The stupid world was unaware of them. Only his rivals in scholarship, a tiny band, were scorched. But the students, revelling in their childish college life, this brood of illiteracy, these ignorant sons of ignoramuses to whom Chaucer was scarcely a name and the bright coruscations of liberated minds no more than meaningless words,—their dull minds were there in the flesh before him! If incapable of knowing what literature was about, they could be made to translate what literature said into their weak vernacular, describe Athene if they could never understand intellectual love, give the meaning of a reference to the Augean stables, if they were incompetent to absorb the line that carried it. With what ironic unction, glaring the while

at us, he used to pronounce the verses of
Dryden—

. . . *That unfeathered two-legged thing, a son,*
Got, while his soul did huddled notions try,
And born a shapeless lump, like anarchy.

This was pure thwarting, and warping, of a
fine mind. It was a scholar's ineffective revenge
upon the anti-intellectualism of college life in
which he, and all he stood for, was meaningless.
Indeed, two vitalities were combatting each other
with no attempt at conciliation on either side.
Our Gothic resistance to ideas and to ideals of
accuracy and right knowledge maddened him.
His Gothic insistence on exact knowledge of subjects which seemed irrelevant to modern life an-
tagonized us. And it was the Gothic blindness
of the college authorities who would not see that
they were setting two cultures, two educations
at each other's throats, which explained such
crimes in the name of education as his students
witnessed daily, wondering that a white beard
could wag so rejoicingly over slaughter. For it
was the least literate, least literary among the
undergraduates that, in those days of compulsory courses, they ordered to attend his place of
sacrifice.

[217]

I may seem to forget the college as a whole in writing of that hybrid out of literature by science called literary scholarship, which was one of its by-products. But the college as a whole was deeply involved. We students and teachers of the modern languages and literatures had succeeded to the place in college education which had been held for centuries by the classicists. But we lacked the classicists' confidence and the classicists' power. They had believed that a real knowledge of the great literatures of Greece and Rome would make an educated man, and, in spite of their overweening, had often been proved right, until the spell of the Renaissance, which for three centuries had made the Western world believe in the magical benefits to be derived from even the grammar of Latin, was broken. We scholars of the Gothic age, substituting the grammar of Chaucer and Milton, the facts of literary history, had changed the dosage without renewing that vital insight into a culture which had made Renaissance teaching and scholarship great. It was a new culture we faced, a new Renaissance in which our most passive student was soon to be flung against the complex forces of industrialism. And these forces we did not

[218]

attempt to relate with the literature which it was our business to teach, because our training in specialized scholarship had made us incapable of anything but skilful antiquarianism. We were afraid of the complex emotionalism of literature, which inevitably relates itself to every new manifestation of human nature, or dies because it has no vital relation. We were afraid without knowing that we were afraid, precisely as the clergymen of our day were afraid without realizing it of religion as such, with its passionate and radical emotionalism. And so we fell back upon dates and sources, or as teachers painfully broke through into a half knowledge of our desperate problem. But as scholars few broke through. Honor to them, but already the books of most are dead on the library shelves, while the little knowledge they contributed to history has been absorbed without noticeable results. One has only to compare the contributions of the scientists in that age with the contributions of literary scholarship to know that something was wrong.

I honor most in my memory, therefore, the great teachers, the personalities who expressed the tension in their minds in their classrooms if not in their books, making the students of the old college uneasily aware of perceptions which science could not give them, and emotions richer than their own college life. Fortunately in those little academic communities, still walled in by privilege and prejudice from the bourgeois industrialism outside, all lived close together, and were curious each to know more of the other's thoughts. They passed daily on the campus:— the candid and simple crew captain; the foxy-eyed boy in pursuit of social prestige; the manager of a team already aware of how pockets were lined; Gibbs meditating theories that were to transform science; Beers shuffling home with Emerson in his heart; deans thinking of new buildings; and the research scholar, annoyed because he must shortly explain Shakespeare to the pink-faced freshman who tipped his hat and hurried on to the gymnasium.

Monasteries at the end of the age of faith must also have had their complexes. Many a young lay brother must have been stirred to wonder, contempt, or a puzzled admiration, at the sight of Anselm at work upon his hundredth copy of a Book of Hours. Some such collision between a new era and a new barbarism with the peaceful world of literary scholarship was responsible for the strains and stresses, the eccentricities, and the futile attempts to exalt the letter at the expense of the spirit, which were so characteristic of scholarship in our college. The erudition was genuine. But it was stunted,—too often inapplicable, incomplete, and as aimless as the money-getting passion of millionaires who enriched themselves while they forgot the art of living for which riches were made.

CHAPTER IX

The Alumni

$\mathcal{A}$ DESCRIPTION of the American college without mention of the alumni would be like a picture of the Golden Throne which left out the heavenly hosts. Those paintings by Tintoretto of the celestial hierarchy surrounded by circle upon circle of the innumerable elect out to the shining margin of space and time, might be regarded as mystic symbols of the collegiate world. The alumni were the saved and the blest, still testifying to the vigor and the virtue of the college; they were like the saints and martyrs of the hierarchies, translated but still powerful. To them it owed a part, and usually the most sumptuous part, of the visible body of buildings, from them came great draughts of financial nourishment, and their opinions, their prejudices, their ideals, and their romanticism, were strong and sometimes determining factors in the academic atmosphere. An American college without its alumni is as hard to imagine as a man without an environment. They were its environment; a conditioning principle always at work.

Although it was not my idea originally, and I forget from whom I borrowed it, yet I give my heartiest endorsement to the theory that the alumni and alumnae bond is one of the most important in the social history of the United States. Our society from the beginning has been heterogeneous and disruptive. The class consciousness (I use the term in an old-style sense) which kept England stable, weakened here as soon as formed. Rank and its prestige, which stiffened society in monarchical Europe, has never been more than a shadow of a shadow in America. Nor have we at any time in our history formed those almost unbreakable bonds of membership in religious societies which lie so close beneath the surface of an otherwise familiar Europe. Not even Catholicism has formed a caste in the United States. In radicalism, too, we have been individualists, cold except for brief moments to revolutionary fraternities. But the inevitable impulse for the like-minded to foregather has operated here as elsewhere. We have the many fraternal organizations such as the Shriners or the Odd Fellows, who obviously have borrowed many of their customs from the college class and the college fraternity. But far surpassing these welfare associations in cohesiveness and in a powerful though more diffused influence upon American *mores,* is the strong bond of graduation from an American college. Of this the college fraternity is only a concentration. It was the shaping of minds and coloring of emotions that made the alumni a conscious class union, although economic status undoubtedly determined the personnel. I write particularly of the men now in their forties and fifties who went to college when going to college was still a privilege, who went to college not in the amorphous droves of the state university but in selected groups attending the typical institution, half private half public, half slave to convention half free to be eccentric and individual, which I have described in previous pages.

I speak of alumni rather than alumnae, but not invidiously. The sorority of women graduates grows in extent as it becomes increasingly conventional for women to go to college, yet it is probably too late for them to feel a class apart. The universities which they now attend in such numbers are too large for the intimate class life of the old college. In the Gothic Age the alumnae were a tiny minority of the population. And they were differently worked upon by the college. Some of them went to college as professionally as we men to graduate or law school, and so never knew the conflict with college life, while the others had a home and husband in view, and so probably never gave themselves as wholeheartedly as their brothers to the life of the college. Here I may be wrong, but certainly women in college in my day were less adolescent, much less romantic, than the men. They were on a by-path away from the women's world, and were aware of it. The men were hot-footing down a main road that everyone knew about and approved. College life left the girls in need of adjustment, but tumbled the boys into a waiting society for which their training exactly fitted them.

Graduating from college in the nineties and early nineteen hundreds was more painful than triumphant. The youth stepped out into the world trailing clouds of memory behind him.

The Alumni

He took on a new identity as clerk, law student, or office assistant, yet held desperately to his affiliation with a caste of men whose memories were like his own. He might work as he was told to work, but he thought, felt, and as far as possible lived, as he had learned to do in college. A difference in the way he handled experience as sensible as his different clothes and different vocabulary, separated him from his old friends in the home town who had not gone to college. He grew more like them, but never just like them. There was always in his mind a reference back to the college, even after thirty years.

Speaking for myself, I remember that I was arrogant without reason and absurd without necessity when I first became an alumnus. Now that the collegiate has become vulgar it is hard to realize how seriously the earlier graduates of the college life undertook their obligations to be unmistakably college men. (No one but the police called them college boys then.) They kept the badinage of college talk, the carelessness of college dress fastidiously applied to rigorously selected garments, most of all the comradeship among their equals in experience. And this comradeship rapidly extended beyond the coterie

[227]

lines of college days, broadening into friendships which might include anyone who had walked the campus in the golden days now becoming historical.

Thus as men and Americans the alumni might be dull, bright, agreeable, cantankerous, radical, conservative, failures or successes, differing as widely as human nature permits within the vague limits of an economic class. But as alumni, while these differences persisted, there was a thin garment of resemblance which covered their personal peculiarities like an academic gown. The alumni retained that quick response to an appeal for loyalty which they had learned in college. There they had acquired faith in an institution, an intangible entity which could not be wrong however much its personnel might wrong them. They kept an instinctive belief in the value of co-operation within a group, which was to be of inestimable advantage to the corporations and foundations of the next twenty years when industrial and philanthropic enterprise grew beyond the power of control by individuals. And much more important than these advantages, which other groups possessed also, they shared a common memory of a vivid and homogeneous experience intelligible to all of them, which, in the restless haphazard life of an America constantly on the move, gave a point of rest and departure. Subtly combined with this was an expectation of success acquired in an institution made up from the select. And outweighing all of these useful assets of the alumni, was one result of college life which only psychologists have appreciated. For with rare exceptions the alumni had been happy in their colleges. Whatever their later disillusions, for the best part of four years they had been content and had, at the very least, learned to believe in the possibility of happiness. Other men, naturally, had been happy in youth, but I can think of no other institution which so successfully generated happiness over a long period and at a time when every youthful faculty was sensitive to impressions. With all its faults and virtues operating together, the college was bound to make a type of the alumnus, and did.

If this seems an exaggeration, contrast the American with the English college. There was the same high level of happiness in England, and a far better education for the intellect. Co-operation, and powerful co-operation, among men of like experience was also a product of those older colleges. But that loyalty which for good and ill became a convention with the American alumnus, in England never got beyond a respect for *alma mater*. The great generosity of the American for his college and his deep affection, have no adequate parallels in England, where there was loyalty to ideals, but no sense of responsibility for the welfare of the college whence those ideals came.

When as alumni we began to come back to *alma mater* for our reunions and talk there of what the college had meant to us and was going to mean to our children, it was not hard to see what we wanted. There was a growing realization of the importance of the curriculum. We were old enough now to appreciate the framework of knowledge which the college had given us, and to know that, sketchy as it was, it had been valuable. But what we remembered best, and solicited its continuance for our own young, was the romance that had suffused our fierce competitions and strenuous enjoyments. We had been the last wave of the romantic movement, and with us it had interpenetrated middle-class materialism. Our loyalty was not to a system of

teaching or a curriculum, but to a way of life.
And it was characteristic of those college generations that the older they grew the more romantic
they became about their college years. Our
memory was of a sacred community whose songs
had not been as other songs, whose teams had
been (and must continue to be) better than other
teams, whose "profs" were more eccentric than
other "profs," whose college spirit was superior
to the spirit of other colleges, and far superior
to anything outside of college. The alumnus
may have lived in a shabby frame house under
a dripping elm tree, but his college life in memory was nevertheless touched with gold.

The first result of his romanticism was im-
pressive and naive. In those Eastern endowed
institutions which set the fashions for college
life, it was the loyal alumni who wiped out
deficits and supplied the funds for new enter-
prises beyond the means of the college budget.
They supported the university, but what they
loved was the little old college within it, which
had been in a true sense their fostering mother.
While great endowments began to reconstruct
the university teaching of medicine and law, in
the college the golden shower was changed to

stone and mortar. Slowly at first but with increasing momentum through the boom years, the bare and nondescript college of my youth began to transform itself into a romantic alumnus's dream of a proper setting for college life. His imagination unfortunately was not strong. If he had seen his college as the 100% American institution it certainly was, he would have ordered his architects to adapt to academic purposes the beautiful simplicity and clarity of the steel, glass, and concrete construction he was erecting outside of the college campus. We should have had a new architecture. But his imagination was antiquarian, and somewhat sentimental. Having fought the curriculum for four years in college, he began belatedly to recognize the value of tradition, perhaps because he came to realize that it was his sense of historical continuity acquired in college that set him apart from ordinary uneducated men. And so, moved by instinct rather than reason, he chose the florid Tudor Gothic style, which I have already mentioned as characteristic of our *fin de siècle*, and remade the college according to his own fancy. It was a style as expensive as his own life was becoming, and in its blend of tradition, imitativeness, sham, and eccentricity, and its uncertain relationship to the America which it has spotted with ramparts, cathedral towers (sometimes very beautiful), gargoyles, machicolations, and light resistant windows, is so characteristic of the college, which welcomed it rapturously, that I have used the word "Gothic" to designate this age of American education.

The alumnus was romantic in other ways. He tried to keep his past intact. It is doubtful whether, as a student, he had ever understood just what his official educators were trying to do for him, unless he had been enrolled in engineering or other applied sciences, in which case he had been regarded as an inferior breed. But he had been vividly aware of the unity of his life, a unity which he now assigned not to the vital relations between college life and the main currents of energy in America, but rather to other influences that as an undergraduate he had rather sniffed at. And so returning to the campus after ten or twenty years, he realized that his social and athletic strenuosities had in some subtle way been given tone by studies he had been forced to make in subjects which had nothing to do with activities of the campus or the business career that came afterward. And he felt that what otherwise might have been only four years of sports and rivalries had been dignified by such disciplines as history, literature, mathematics even, which made his adolescent experiences a part of the historical experience of memorable men as far back as the Greeks, and gave margins to life that made him different from uneducated barbarians.

Hence the alumnus became an educational conservative, how powerful an influence presidents and trustees know, if professors do not. He might insist that "practical" courses in his own technical field (if he had one) should be introduced into his old college, because, thanks to his loyalty, he hoped to recruit his industry from recent graduates of his own *alma mater*. Yet talk to him at reunion or other revisitings of the academic shades, and you would find him arguing for the old "culture" that made gentlemen, by which he usually meant the Greek he had flunked in freshman year, or the literature he had escaped from with a C;—for the old professors who left such indelible memories of unworldly personality behind them;—and even for an extension of the old subjects to the exclusion of new scientific nonsense:—Latin, Greek, classic history, and courses (here he searched his memory) on Shakespeare, Napoleon, Dante, Beowulf, George Washington, or the Augustan age, which gave a man something about which he could talk. Such new subjects as government, economics, psychology, which have more than anything else brought the college of today into touch with the problems as well as the financial opportunities of modern life, did not interest him. What he wanted, what aroused his enthusiasm when he found it still existed was (quite rightly) whatever strengthened character as he had seen it strengthened he knew not exactly how or why; and next an education that gilded the profit-making system and made it fit for gentlemen.

Nevertheless, the American alumnus is one of the really engaging figures of social history. In his function of elder brother to the college he has not always been admirable, but likable he has always been. I saw in my own experience his romantic enthusiasm for "our team" become a country-wide passion which came near to making athletics the chief purpose of so-called higher education. Like children wanting one more exciting story before bedtime, the alumni demanded victories until intercollegiate play was expanded into a professional entertainment which has slaughtered more than one educational ideal to make a November holiday. It was this crude confusion of the methods of business with the aims of education that drove many a college president to justify professional sports by their advertising value. Yet it was these same alumni who poured in not only their millions, but their little tens and fives, to make their college into a university, and their university into something which they themselves often neither liked nor understood.

Now loyalty is a quality which doubtless has done as much harm as good, and which certainly is the most easily misled of all the virtues. Yet, like strength of body or of mind, it must always command respect, no matter whence it flows, or what it furthers. The alumni, though they spoke of *alma mater*, acted like the loyal parents of a puzzling child. Criticism of the old college, often violent and sometimes virulent, was the staple of alumni conversation. But there was always an underlying assumption that we were attacking men and measures, not the college as it had been and might be. Realistic criticism which disputed the value of the institution itself or of the kind of education which could be got there, left us cold or angry. Unless one believed, as we believed, in college life, reform could mean only destruction.

Other loyalties, to church, to moral codes, to country, and even to family life, were being sadly shaken in the years when the alumni became so numerous as to constitute a class. Hence this one devotion which kept its intensity and its romance was of considerable social importance. If it made dreamers and sentimentalists, and sometimes foes to progress, of some college graduates, it also steadied them all and unquestionably sweetened their lives. In the rather drab small-town and sordid city of the early twentieth century, this enduring college relationship was an alleviation not to be despised.

Yet this affection for *alma mater* led to one of the ironies of educational history. The rivers of money which poured in for every college purpose in the golden Gothic age, did not always or even often come from far-sighted patrons of education, but were the gifts, incredibly numerous, and sometimes incredibly large, of plain college graduates who loved their college, or of outsiders impressed by the glamour of college life. This stream had a sacrificial quality. Some of it, of course, went into Bowls and Stadiums, where the alumni with numerous companions who had never smelled a sheep-skin revived their youth by yelling themselves into a bronchitis. These vast structures, as the undergraduates' interest in professionalized athletics diminishes, begin here and there to lift their half-empty bulks like the ruined amphitheatres of the Roman empire. And still more flowed into memorial buildings of collegiate Gothic, where it was not the pardonable memorializing of a family name that was significant, but the expense in proportion to the usefulness and the beauty achieved. But a larger, a much larger sum still, was given direct to the beloved college, for its own purposes, whatever they might be. It was thus that a Syracusan king gave vases of gold and statues of cunning bronze to the shrine at Delphi for the memorializing of a god.

Here loyalty had a strange reward. This money, uncritically and lovingly given in memory of college life, has destroyed college life as we knew it, even in the new housing plans devised to keep some of the old intimacies. It has

made the college into a university, the university into a factory of research. Romance has fled and irresponsibility grows unfashionable. It has substituted for the old-fashioned professor who touched our imaginations rather than our minds, a new professor, realist, member of a brain trust, efficient, aware that university education now must really educate, and who makes it do so at the expense of many pleasant amenities. And for the campus, a community with its own customs and its own happiness, it has substituted a congeries of schools, where even the undergraduates are in increasing numbers hard working, hard thinking, and able and willing to relate their studies to the actualities of American life. Such rigorous education does not come until it is needed. It may be said that in the age of confidence we did not indispensably need it. But now that it is needed, it is the alumni of the old college who have paid the bill. As the old college was a preparatory school for the competitions of the early 1900's, so the new university is a laboratory in which the problems of the later decades of the twentieth century are being studied by experts. Those who contributed to the rebuilding of the ancient nest find an office building waiting for them when they return. Not even the Tudor Gothic trimmings, concessions to their romanticism, can hide that fact. The old college has gone—for better or worse. I personally should say for both.

It is probable that many of the traits which have made the twentieth century American in business and the professions a strongly marked national type, recognizable as such throughout the world, are really traits of the alumni of the old American colleges. We Americans should have become in these decades more, not less, European, for since the Civil War a vast immigration has flooded in everywhere except the South, modifying the physical type, especially in the cities. And yet the typical reactions of the country in morals, politics, religion, and economics have remained characteristically un-European, and better explained by the American past, than by an Italian-American or German-American present. This stabilizing of character and temperament, and also of prejudice, is probably due to the college graduate, for our alumni strengthened their bonds and gained in class consciousness just when the so-called old American was losing his grip.

The Alumni

This broadcasting of college traits by the unorganized but powerful influence of the alumni, may explain some characteristics of our recent history which have puzzled Europeans. A good example is the curious tenacity with which Americans have held on to democratic ideals in a country where business has been autocratic. It was in college that our alumni learned to respect democracy while keeping it within strict limits. There the underdog was welcomed when he fought his way up, which, if not pure democracy, is certainly on its doorstep. A college reunion beautifully illustrates this faith in democracy when, and if, it works. After twenty or thirty years, privilege, prestige, and progress have all had their chance to make or remake the fortunes of a college class. Socially these returning men have stratified, economically their fate is usually determined. Here are the results of the big game of half a lifetime posted for anyone to see. Nobodies have become somebodies, somebodies have remained just somebodies, and by a rough justice everyone seems to have got just about what was coming to him—what his personality and his character deserved quite as much as what his privileges or lack of them made probable. The initial handicap of economic inferiority had been too much for some to overcome; early and easy success had been as great a handicap for others. Some of the "big men" of college days were still outstanding, but not all; some of the unknown, the freaks and the grinds, had come through, but some only. There was quite enough evidence of success for the deserving to justify the belief of the graduate that his brand of democracy had worked, and that there should be a road to opportunity, kept open if rocky, at least for collegiate America.

And still other traits of contemporary America may be traced back to the college. The outstanding characteristic of American policy in the last two decades has been its violent inconsistency. Look at it. An extraordinary organization for the war in 1917-1918; and a complete disorganization in the handling of the peace. An incomparably efficient organization of industry in the boom decade; and an almost complete anarchy of business and financial control of that boom, ending in an unparalleled smash. A magnificent extension of philanthropy and science applied to humanitarian ends, extending beyond our boundaries around the world; and a failure, almost complete, to organize a radical reform of our own social ills, although every corrupt municipal government and depressed agricultural community has been flying flags of distress. The most elaborate school system in the world; and the highest percentage of crime. Wealth so great that it had to be given away; and inexplicable poverty, less desperate but even more destructive, than the poverty of Europe.

For all this there were many causes, but one at least was the education of our alumni, the dominant college class. They had learned to compete but not to analyze; they had learned to co-operate but not to seek long-term ends; they had been given faith in their own membership but, in spite of the Sumners, no real conception of society as a whole. They had been powerfully educated to make themselves successful in an aggressive, unscrupulous, competitive community, and less powerfully to gild their success with some approach toward fine living. But of the strong laws of cause and effect (except in applied science and trading), and of the great debate as to what makes a civilization, how it can be attained, and conserved, they had little knowledge, for their thoughts were never turned that way.

It is the college alumni that by character, tenacity, loyalty, and will, have held together a centrifugal America, and will hold it together certainly for a little while yet. The virtues of the old college were sound, yet not enough to raise greater expectations than this of its graduates. The small-town campus as we knew it, with its narrow class consciousness, and its easy terms for success, was not an environment which could make the alumnus add hard thinking to his equipment of instinctive reactions. Longfellow's old ship of state that we used to urge to "sail on" from schoolboy platforms begins to yaw and jibe. It is time to quit squabbling over her payroll and set a course. And this requires navigation, a subject which in its broader implications we were never taught in college. And would have passed off with a night's cramming if it had been assigned to us.

CHAPTER X

A State Within a State

ONE of the characteristics of the academic life in the Gothic Age of America was a tendency to preach, and indeed if our best teachers had lived in the seventeenth century they would have published sermons instead of research and criticism. In my last chapter I have given way to this inbred desire to turn history into ideas and prophecy. I believe that our alumni are the inevitable product of the college community as I knew it; yet no one can say with assurance how later history will describe their role today —whether it is reactionary or stabilizing or (as I believe) both. Yet whether important or not for a posterity that perhaps concerns me more than it should, this alumni body is certainly important for us because it still controls the colleges and the education of our children.

This book, however, is not written about the

future, or even the present, except by implication. It deals with the college world as it was, for itself. That campus community has now drifted back in time beyond the complexities of the post-war age. It is clear, now, as I have said before, that it was a state within the state. In every culture there has been a state within the state, and a struggle, covert or open, between those who wish to learn before living, and those who will not be deterred from the immediacy of life. Plato and the Venerable Bede and Erasmus were partisans in such a conflict, and the ambidextrous Napoleon tried to take both sides at once. The test of a good life is neither content while living it, since content may be either gross or stolid, nor success which results from it, since success is precarious and so differently measured. A more satisfactory criterion is the vividness of the experience, particularly when the memory persists afterward, and is pleasurable through good times and bad. That vividness the conflict of ideas within the college certainly gave, and students and faculty, each in their own way, shared its intensity.

A dozen different and better ways than ours might have been devised for educating the dominant class of twentieth century America, but would any of them have worked better? I doubt it. We students were the irresistible upwash of a century of material progress; we were the seventh wave and strongest flowing from the turbulent exploiting of a continent morally exhausted by the Civil War. If we had found a society of perfect scholars, or radical realists, or inflexible conservers of tradition in the college, we, with the alumni behind us, would have washed them out. Our faculties were creatures of the age that made us. They fought us, often with a vigor as intense if less romantic than our own strenuosity; yet they were as inconsistent in their secret respect for our energy of materialism, as we were naive in our faith that such perfect confidence as ours must conquer all difficulties.

But indeed, if I shift my point of view from student to professor, it begins to seem a little romantic to have been teaching the undergraduate at a time when the college life was so powerfully conditioning the next generation of characteristic Americans. It is exciting to consider how right we were in insisting to our hungry classes that man does not live by bread alone, or in laying down cold postulates of logic which, if valid,

meant that the wild chase they were about to
enter was headed for the Gadarene cliff. It is
humiliating to remember how wrong were our
methods, how feeble our compromises, how muddled our own minds. As martyrs for wisdom's
sake we put on a poor show in that college circus.
We rather enjoyed seeing our own colleagues
thrown to the lions of Philistinism, and, if we
went down into the arena ourselves, kept a door
labelled "Common Sense" or "What's the Use"
half open behind us in case the beasts became
really dangerous. Still, by and large, even if our
doctrine was uncertain, we kept the faith. Our
embattled teaching was quite as American in
tradition and spirit as the get-rich-quick ideas of
our students. We kept hammering away in spite
of discouragement and frustration at what we
variously thought was education—Latin sub-
junctives, the binomial theorem, Plato's Republic, the second law of thermodynamics,
Tennyson's morality, the sheer beauty of Keats,
the meaning of God in an industrial civilization,
the difference between meaning and a word.

And this all happened in a tight little community—in self-contained little communities
scattered all over the country and each a self-

conscious society within the larger framework of the nation. Yet we were unlike the equivalent academies of Greece or the universities of the Middle Ages, in that they were a terminal where men met to settle if possible the meaning of their lives, whereas our society was strictly preparatory. For the college was not then a center of thought like the new universities of this century, but primarily a nursery and testing ground for youth, where much that was said and most that was done, looked forward not to *the* future, but to *a* future for the boy who then and there was preparing for active life. This accounts for the narrowness of our education, but made it bite deep into the emotions, quite as deep as the grip upon character and behavior of the intellectually still more limited English public schools.

There was a class of the redoubtable Sumner's which I attended every Monday morning. The old man sat, as always, slouched on a chair upon the dais. I do not remember that he ever spoke standing. He had no oratory; his eyes were always fixed on some vacancy over our heads as he lectured in a gruff voice that did not rise or fall, and which depended upon the pith and substance of what was said for its holding power.

It was the first lecture after a Spring week-end. A roar of talk went round the seats, subduing as the clock struck the hour into the rustle of a hundred newspapers. As he began, looking more than ever like Cato on a monument, his voice was scarcely audible, but his first words beat down the confusion of sound. "When I wish to speak through newspapers, I do it by correspondence," he said grimly, pausing until the sarcasm went home. The front rows snickered, but since no further witticism followed, began to whisper again. "I was to lecture to you young gentlemen," he continued, "on the danger of taxing the strong for the benefit of the weak." He paused. I believe that the smug innocence of our sunburnt week-end faces roused some pity in his realist mind, and certainly it must have been the careless inattention of those polite but indifferent youngsters, holding their newspapers half masted while they rested perfunctory pencils on their open notebooks, that made him personal for once. "You pay no taxes. You are as yet neither weak nor strong, for you are dependents. Your first test will be earning a living, your next marriage. You think you will succeed in both. I can tell you that statistically considered not four

in ten of your marriages will be truly successful.
They will fail (I hope my memory quotes him
accurately) because you are too ignorant of the
real values of living to make them succeed.
Gentlemen, you will not find that statement in
the newspapers you are reading." They dropped
them hastily, yet the next morning the statement
was in the newspapers—characteristically shifted
into sensationalism: "Sumner says marriage in
America a failure."

That incident seems to sum up my conception
of our college. The confident, healthy indifference of the student body, so self-absorbed in their
hour, so easy to capture for an idea, so sure to
escape from its implications. And also the defeatism of a first-rate mind in the face of this
impregnable youth, which could be shown again
and again the way and the truth, but did not
want that way or any truth, but only to live.
Youth impervious to the winds of doctrine, yet
happily at least made aware that there are winds
and that they may blow.

I will add to this brief instance of the mood
and temper of the day two college biographies
which illustrate better than argument the quality
of this academic atmosphere which, like the light

of special lands such as Greece, had a power of transfiguration, which often made illusion but was always glamorous.

I knew Everett first as a freshman, a boy singularly courteous, who in the classroom was always helpful, even when his not too brilliant brains missed the point of a question. He was one of those youths who seem waiting for the world to use them, co-operative, unselfish, kind. Chance brought us together outside the lecture hall, and I became his friend and could follow his career. It was almost too successful at first. He came from a fine school and he was both good looking and athletic. As his mind was well trained his courses did not worry him. Easily and inevitably he was drawn into extracurriculum activities, first as an apprentice then as a principal. He was on a committee of the Y. M. C. A., left end of the football team, assistant manager of the daily paper, the kind of student the dean sent for whenever something was going wrong on the campus. Although his marks did not suffer, his mind became a hotel room for the transaction of the business of college life. With him there were no ulterior motives. He liked success, but did not go after it. What he enjoyed was doing

what others were doing; if he had any other impulse it was pure loyalty to his class and college.
He really believed that when he played football,
settled a college row, or brought more recruits to
the Y. M. C. A., he was most serviceable to his
college, and that gave him deep pleasure.

I saw his character round out and harden, felt
also that his mind was growing more and more
inflexible.   To do something for *that*—to
decline his calls to service in order to study and
think, would have seemed to him selfish.   His job
was to keep the college going, not to play with
his own brains in a corner.

Then he had a conversion for which I was not
responsible.   I knew him too well, liked his type
too much for what it was, and was much too
skeptical of changing it, to harrow his conscience
with private attacks on his set of values.   He
knew what I thought, or at least what I said in
public.   But someone else drove a sudden plough
through the quite undisturbed turf of convention
which covered his mind.   It was junior year, and
almost too late, yet he had an awakening.   History engaged him.   Suddenly he saw himself as a
tiny boat rowing madly through a patch of light
on a dark ocean.   He wanted to know, he wanted

to read voluminously, he wanted time to reflect. The apparatus was all there, a library across the campus, hour upon hour of time if he chose to take it, advisers inside the classroom and out, and a certain reward in faculty approval.

He plunged in; but they came to him in mid October, pleading, reproaching, cursing him, because he would not come out for the team. He was fed up with football, and knew that after football came the track team, and with one yielding many. But he gave in. He could not put what he regarded as his private interest ahead of what everyone seemed to regard as his public duties. After a wrench or two the disappointment was not vital. He became one of the acknowledged leaders of his senior class; even the President praised him as a typical product of the best of all colleges—as he was. His brief flare of intellectual interest, like a young girl's amorousness, was soon over. He became a useful citizen, perhaps happier, perhaps more useful, than if he had persisted in trying to find out what it was all about.

Everett's story seems to me neither a tragedy of college life, nor a triumph. It is merely an instance of the muddle of values in that Gothic college, and of the power of college life; it is a proof of how much better than the state outside it nourished loyalty and encouraged disinterested action, and of how it failed only in *lux et veritas*.

My other instance is of a young instructor whom I knew intimately, and whose career sometimes paralleled and sometimes diverged widely from my own. He was a shy man with a gift for teaching which he nursed into a talent, though at the expense of many tossing nights, and shaking voice and hands in his first class-rooms. But his genius was for discovery. Documents that everyone had missed tumbled into his hands. Theories evolved in his fertile brain seemed always to find facts to support them. Before he was thirty-two he had published one book and a dozen articles.

Nevertheless the breaks were against him. He had not been elected to the proper societies in college, nor was his brilliance the kind which takes a Phi Beta Kappa key. As a student he had always read too much in the wrong books. This, and his facile mind quick to the point of stuttering, made him as a young instructor suspect to his superiors. His last discovery, his latest theory was felt always to be specious and probably unsound, and by the time their validity had been established to the satisfaction of the faculty table at the club, there was always a new article in print, too clever by far, and certain proof that his engine was running on air.

But he soon had to give up production, since for two years he was ordered to take excess teaching because of the illness of a colleague and the sudden departure of another. At the end of that time, a junior in the department, who had just published a solid book with no dubious ideas in it, was promoted over his head, on the ground that the college needed men who were contributing to knowledge. His recourse was to seek a job elsewhere, but he had printed nothing for two years so that it was natural for outsiders to suppose that his promise had been delusive.

He had a wife and two children. If, almost by accident, he had not discovered that he could lecture acceptably to women's clubs, they would have been passing poor on $3000 a year, which in a blocked department was all he could count upon through an indefinite future. But these extra-curriculum earnings were, of course, held against him professionally. If he could please the gross public, it seemed improbable that he was a real scholar.

He had two alternatives. He could bide his time, get to work, and wait for an opportunity, which then could not, perhaps, be denied him. Or he could try to force an issue. And here came into the problem that curious difference between the campus and the world outside. He was willing to be poor, but he was not willing to suffer in prestige by being grouped with those who had failed. He asked for a professorship, with no increase in salary. Twice it was refused him. The third time, thanks to a sense that his persistence was in accord with a proper academic ambition, he got it. There was also an uneasy feeling that perhaps he was really brilliant in a department that had specialized in dull, sound men.

He got his professorship; and died of it two years later. For his professorial responsibility brought rounds of committee meetings, while in the time that was left from routine, having cut out lecturing, he tried desperately to show his college that he was not unworthy of the confidence they had displayed in giving him a title without a salary. There were three children now, less money, and more worry. He died in the course of the struggle, and is remembered as the most promising young man in his field in his time.

It was surely the *mores* of the academic world that wrecked him. The college gave the opportunity, priceless to a mind like his, to do what he loved best; and the college by its timorousness, by its narrow loyalties, by its insistence that students and teachers alike should play the game according to the rules laid down in a jealous and self-contained community, the college surely killed this fine-bladed spirit.

Thus and thus in the consulship of Plancus (as Beers called an earlier and perhaps more truly golden age) did we live and have our being, and fail or succeed, not often knowing why. It must have been a rich experience, since in reading biographies I find records of like intensity only in the stories of the pioneers. That for student, teacher, scholar it was a deeply conditioning experience, perhaps needs no more argument. It has never had its Walt Whitman, yet the Americans that came out of it are as strongly marked, and historically quite as important, as his democratic brotherhood of the workers. Although they were diverse in origin like the first immigrants to our shores, yet all were conscious of certain standards, all had a memory of happiness, or at the least of energies fully exerted, all had a belief in that intangible entity, the college spirit, which I have tried to define in this book. And if turning in retrospect from some misty and I fear highly disagreeable decade of the latter twentieth century, the social historian of that day seeks to know what the nineties, the nineteen hundreds, the nineteen tens were like in his America, he should not forget the college town, the dormitories elm-shaded, the campus where two philosophies of living saluted in passing and sometimes stopped for a chat. As a contribution to a history which will some day be written, I, as an alumnus of *alma mater*, have here set down my own memories of this Gothic Age, which are critical, speculative, but most of all affectionate.

THE END